Kursk 1943

The Greatest Tank Battle in History

Kursk 1943

The Greatest Tank Battle in History

N. KAMPOURIS - G. ZOURIDIS - I. THEODORATOS - D. STAVROPOULOS
J. VARSAMIS - S. VOURLIOTIS - D. GEDEON - S. VALMAS

Illustrated by J. Shumate, V. Auletta, D. Hadoulas

'Escape from Hell, Kursk 1943' by Johnny Shumate.

AUTHORS
N. Kampouris - G. Zouridis - I. Theodoratos
D. Stavropoulos - J. Varsamis - S. Vourliotis
D. Gedeon - S. Valmas

EDITOR (ENGLISH EDITION)
Stelios Demiras

TRANSLATOR
Alexis Mehtidis

PROOF EDITOR
Charles Davis

COVER ART AND UNIFORM RESEARCH-ILLUSTRATIONS
Johnny Shumate

AIRCRAFT PROFILES
Vincenzo Auletta

AFV PROFILES
Dimitris Hadoulas

ART DIRECTOR AND COVER DESIGN
Dimitra Mitsou

MAPS
Dimitra Mitsou

PICTURE CREDITS
Bundesarchive, US Archives, Authors' Archives,
Periscopio Publications' Collection

First published in Greece in 2009
by Periscopio Publications
in cooperation with Squadron/Signal Publications

Distributed worldwide exclusively
by Squadron/Signal Publications
1115 Crowley Drive
Carrollton, TX 75006-1312 U.S.A.
www.SquadronSignalPublications.com

© 2009 Periscopio Publications

ISBN: 978-089747569-3

DIMITRIOS STAVROPOULOS
Dimitrios Stavropoulos is a graduate mechanical engineer and works in the Greek defense industry. He has published a series of articles on military history since 1996 and has edited 20 books in the Greek language.

STAVROS VALMAS
Stavros Valmas was born in Athens, Greece in 1964. Educated in the US (Arizona State University), he has a B.Sc. in Industrial Engineering and one in Business Administration. He is Logistics Manager for a major metals manufacturer in Greece and has traveled extensively around Europe to visit military museums. These visits have afforded him a large picture collection. His main area of interest is World War II German and Soviet land and air equipment. Currently, he is building up his Desert Storm photo collection.

SOTIRIS VOURLIOTIS
Sotiris Vourliotis was born in Athens in 1968. He studied in the Department of Mechanical Engineering of the Chalkis Technological Educational Institution and then in the School of Mechanical Engineering of the National Technical University of Athens. He works as a public works designer. He has written articles for the Periscopio Publications' military history and defence magazines since 2000 and has dealt with various subjects, mostly of the World War II period, in which he has been interested since his school years.

DIMITRIOS GEDEON
Dimitrios Gedeon is a Major General (retired). He is a graduate of Hellenic Army Military Academy (Class of 1960) and Hellenic Armed Forces National Defense School. He served in the Hellenic Army from 1960 to 1989 and has been a teacher of Military History in the Hellenic Army Military Academy from 1994 to 1997, Assistant Director of the Hellenic Army History Directorate and Secretary to the Hellenic Military History Commission from 1997 to 1999. He has written two books about Hellenic Army History and a great number of articles on Military History.

GEORGE ZOURIDIS
George Zouridis was born in Athens, Greece in 1955. He studied at the Athens University of Economics and Business, graduating in 1978. Graduate studies followed in Boston, USA, from where he acquired a Master in Economics. Zouridis has been dealing with the study of modern and contemporary history for more than 20 years and has been contributing to Periscopio Publications since 1998. He has written several articles as well as alternative history scenarios about World War II. He has also written *The October Revolution 1917* for Periscopio Publications.

IOANNIS THEODORATOS
Ioannis Theodoratos was born in Athens in 1965. He is an historian researcher, journalist and also Editor in chief of the magazines "Military History" and "Hellenic Defense Review," which are published in Greek. He also teaches military history, and geopolitics-geostragy issues of the Greek and global history in the College "Elliniki Agogi" in Athens.

JOHN VARSAMIS
John Varsamis was born in Athens in 1973. He graduated from the National Technical University of Athens as a chemical engineer and then obtained his Master's Degree in Business and Administration from the Athens School of Economics and Business. He has long been a researcher on WWII. He has been writing for Periscopio Publications since 1993, and is the author of the following books on WW II: Axis Fighters, Allied Fighters Volumes A and B, Axis Tanks, and Junkers Ju 87 Stuka (all in Greek).

Contents

A 30cm Nebelwerfer prepares to launch in support of Model's attack on 6 July. With these weapons the Germans, like the Russians with their 'Katyusha' launchers, could deliver a heavy and concentrated barrge. Not the least frightful aspect of the German weapon was the noise it made as it 'rocketed' through the air. Its relative light weight and mobility compared to conventional artillery made it a very effective weapon. (Bundesarchiv)

Preface

In the summer of 1943, after two years of total war on the Eastern Front, the Germans were ready to meet the Soviets on the decisive battlefield.

The German Army, after having been repulsed before its main goal, Moscow and after having been bled white in the great debacle of Stalingrad, had recovered and was all powerful. Finally equipped with new, capable weapons, it was poised for the attack on the salient of Kursk, confident that it would -this time- gain its elusive victory.

However, the new leadership of the Red Army, having gained precious experience and an incontestable numerical superiority in both men and equipment, together with the renowned stubborness of the Soviet troops, posed an insurmountable problem for the Germans.

The greatest tank battle of all time proved to be the beginning of the end for the Third Reich. The elite panzer formations were decimated and would never again regain their former strength.

Nothing could turn the fortunes of war for the Axis and the Soviet flood was not to be stopped until the ruins of Berlin.

Nikos Giannopoulos
Historian

The Rebirth of the Soviet Army

On 2 July 1943, Hitler addressed German troops on the eastern front as they waited to launch the massive summer assault: "This attack will be decisive. It must definitely succeed, quickly and totally. Our victory at Kursk will become a beacon to light the whole world."

Soviet T-34 Model 1943 medium tank, 41st Guards Tank Brigade, 7th Mechanized Corps, Kursk, 1943. The slogan "For Soviet Moldavia" is inscribed on the turret. The white stripe on the turret was an aerial recognition sign. The tank had an overall Dark Green finish. (Illustration by Dimitris Hadoulas/ Historical Notes by Stelios Demiras)

Hitler's words betrayed the sense of urgency with which the Führer and the German High Command (OKW) viewed the impending battle with the Soviet forces. The Nazi leader already realised that time was against them and that they needed an immediate, overwhelming victory to reinforce the morale on the home front, as well as among Germany's allies, where signs of doubt were beginning hesitantly to appear. National Socialist Germany would try to regain the initiative in the war in the East through a major victory at Kursk. The Führer was among those optimists who believed that a new, overwhelming blow against the Red Army could topple the Soviet regime. Most pragmatists hoped at least for a clear victory that would chalk up enough military and political gains to earn the Reich some time to catch its breath.

Indeed, their optimism was not without foundation. The Kursk Salient was, in fact, a golden opportunity to undertake a large encircling operation. If the *Wehrmacht* could cut off and destroy considerable Soviet forces, Germany would be able to regain its balance. A large proportion of German losses had been replaced and new, improved weapons had dramatically increased the *Wehrmacht's* firepower. The Germans hoped for a repetition of their huge summer successes of the two previous years – even if on a smaller scale. They had extensive experience in such operations and they believed that their troops and matériel were still superior to those of the enemy. These hopes would be dashed in a most painful, direct way.

Many Germanophile historians and analysts of World War II, whether intentionally or otherwise, tend to present the Battle of Kursk more as a "limited" or "tactical" German failure than as a Soviet victory. They stress that the battle's outcome was influenced by external factors, including Hitler's impatience and the Allied landings on Sicily, and they tend to avoid recognition of the Red Army's role, regarding it as of secondary importance

SOVIET ARMY SNIPER, KURSK 1943
She wears a camouflage coverall (green and black patches) over standard uniform (not visible here); the 1943 pattern *gimnastyorka* (shirt-tunic) with stand up collar and shoulder boards in khaki color, *sharovary* (trousers) in same color with "semi-breeches" with diamond-shaped reinforcing patch at the knee. She also wears black leather boots and *pilotka* (side cap). She is armed with a 7.62mm Mosin Nagant 1891/30 rifle with PU telescopic sight. (Illustration by Johnny Shumate / Historical Notes-Comments by Stelios Demiras)

to the battle's outcome. In fact, nothing could be further from the truth.

The Soviet Army had, indeed, proved to be extremely vulnerable and inept, compared to the skill demonstrated by the *Wehrmacht* during the preceding years. Despite the courage and endurance of the Russian soldier, the Red Army's evident shortcomings on a command level and the shortages and low quality of the available war matériel, led to tragic disasters. Even when the Soviets were successful, they frequently were unable to follow up those initial successes (e.g. during the Great Winter Counteroffensive of 1941 and after the victory at Stalingrad). The Soviets had, however, shown an outstanding capacity to learn from their mistakes and failures. At Kursk, the Germans expected to confront the same massive but inept and rigid opponent they had overcome time and time again. But in the summer of 1943 they were to meet a completely transformed Red Army.

The deeper, more fundamental transformation of the Soviet Army had to do with its own leadership. Stalin's pre-war Great Purge had deprived the Red Army of large numbers of experienced specialist officers. The Soviets experienced successive disasters in the early years of the war due to a rigid command structure that discouraged personal initiative and allowed no freedom of movement. Officers with experience and knowledge of the art of war had been replaced by "experts" in brandishing political slogans. Yet, a new generation of leaders was gradually emerging from the cauldron of battle, officers who had gained valuable experience from the tough, painful lessons taught by the *Wehrmacht* on the battlefield for two full years. Many of the strategically ineffectual commanders at the beginning of the war had been replaced

or simply lost in battle or, at times, banished to the Siberian GULags, victims of their own errors and their professional ineptitude.

Young, daring, dynamic officers, forged in the fire of war and tempered by hard experience, replaced them. A continuously increasing sense of professionalism permeated all ranks of the Soviet leadership, right down to the lowest levels of the company and platoon. The average age of the top Soviet commanders had fallen by almost 20 years, making them more efficient and energetic. This combination of a young leadership with actual experience in the war soon produced results that showed not only in staff work but, predominantly, in the tactical competence of the troops. During 1942, the Red Army had suffered a decay that almost reached levels of disintegration due to the loss of a large proportion of its better trained troops. But the survivors acquired actual war experience every day and by 1943, the Red Army had managed to remedy its situation and was offering better training to the new units.

The continuously increasing self-confidence and trust of the Soviets in their combat skills had an immediate impact on the troops' morale. This morale boosting went hand-in-hand with the durable strengthening and the ever-increasing size of the Red Army. It had around 16,500,000 men under arms by the beginning of July 1943. This manpower situation, however, was running up against specific shortages in matériel, as the growing army had to make do with a large pool of outdated, obsolete weapons. More than 1/3 of the available 10,000 tanks were of a light type with dubious battlefield effectiveness. Soviet industry, however, had reorganized its production to concentrate on building fewer yet more reliable weapon systems.

The Soviet forces had reorganized on all levels, beyond just the strengthening of troop numbers and equipment. The infantry had suffered tremendous casualties during the previous years. The Red Army was bouncing back but manpower remained an acute problem and the new infantry divisions were much smaller compared to those of 1941, or even those of 1942, consisting of 9,380 men each (compared to the 1941 divisional strength of 14,500). In addition, infantry divisions were extremely weak in artillery support. On the other hand, they were supplied with a large number of automatic weapons, heavy infantry weapons, anti-tank guns, and signals equipment, in order to compensate for this disadvantage. Whenever possible, special emphasis was placed on tough, in-depth training of the troops, who had demonstrated their stoicism many times over.

The armored forces had also grown significantly stronger. All mechanized infantry and tank corps now had organic artillery, anti-tank, mortar, engineer, and signals units. Five new élite tank armies, under the direct control of the high command, had been formed by the summer of 1943. Each fielded two tank corps and one mechanized infantry corps. Special efforts were made to equip these new formations exclusively with T-34 tanks, although large numbers of older vehicles remained in service. The KV-1 tanks had been formed into independent "breakthrough" regiments. There were also sufficient British and American tanks available, although the Soviets did not hold them in high esteem and only grudgingly used them to replace casualties. They were expecting the Germans to use new, improved tank types, as they were already aware of the Tiger I's existence. The discovery of the new German tank

in November 1942 had, justifiably, caused much anxiety among the Soviet staff. Up-gunning the T-34 with the 85mm gun was an improvised measure to counter the new threat, but this new variant was not made available until the end of 1943. While the Soviets slightly outnumbered the Germans, they were still using inferior equipment. Mass production of the SU-76 and SU-85 self-propelled guns had not yet started, so the Soviets were forced to field just the SU-122 and SU-152 assault guns at Kursk. The SU-152 was the only armored vehicle in the Soviet arsenal able to stand against the German behemoths, but they were only available in limited numbers. The Soviets had placed high hopes in the improved organization and training of their armored fighting vehicle (AFV) crews, although they knew only too well that the their matériel was of inferior quality. On the other hand, the introduction of radios in the majority of the tanks in use, and the general improvement in communications had noticeably improved the units' coordination and their tactical flexibility. Moreover, the setting up of repair and maintenance units and their introduction into the structure of the large armored formations had increased both their effectiveness and their capability to operate and survive. The Red Army continued to lack motorized transport, but as huge numbers of American trucks became available, the situation drastically improved, particularly for the armored formations. By mid-1943, around 183,000 of these trucks had been delivered from the USA and Canada. These deliveries went a long way to solving the huge problems facing the Red Army's transport and supply sectors.

One field where the Red Army had dramatically increased its firepower was artillery. Soviet industry had managed not only to replace destroyed matériel, taking into account that almost all pre-war matériel had been lost by 1942, but had done so a number of times over. New, improved gun and howitzer types had been put into service, with the emphasis on 122mm and 152mm calibres. Anti-tank and anti-aircraft artillery had also been improved, as was the Soviets' beloved weapon, the multiple rocket launcher, the *Katyusha*.

The most important improvement in the artillery, however, was organizational. Anti-tank guns were formed into brigades, each equipped with 60 to 75 guns of predominantly 76mm but also including 57mm weapons that were placed under the command of corps and armies. The medium and heavy artillery were formed into divisions. By mid-1943, 26 such formations were combat-ready. Sixteen of these had been designated as "breakthrough" artillery divisions, each grouping together as many as 350 122mm to 203mm guns. The high command attached these formations to armies with the mission of covering the vital sectors with the maximum possible density of fire. These artillery divisions were given extensive support, mostly in communications, which drastically increased their accuracy, speed, and fire coordination. Each frontline army group also fielded more than one anti-aircraft artillery division.

Logistical support, a crucial sector, had also improved beyond all measure. The American canned foods that continuously reached the front were as important as the mobility that American trucks afforded the troops. The vast size of the Soviet forces and the paucity of communications were a major issue when planning and executing operations. This issue would have been harder to resolve if the individual Russian soldier had not been used to fighting and surviving with infinitely less logistical support than other Western armies enjoyed. A Russian soldier could survive in situations where others would have starved to death. The Red Army's "primitivism" was an unusual advantage, as it made it more fast-moving than others, taking into account the means it used, that is, its very low demand on supplies. A re-born Red Army, tough and resolute after two years of a merciless conflict, waited with faith and determination to take the leading role on the Eastern Front.

By mid-1943, the Soviet Union and its leadership could look to the future with optimism. Having managed to bear the brunt of the battle against world's finest war machine for two consecutive years, they had ensured their country's survival and had laid the foundations for the reversal of the situation that would, eventually, take the troops of the Red Army to the heart of the Third Reich.

Russian SU-122 tank destroyer, 5th Guards Tank Army, Kursk, July 1943. The SU-122 was the Soviet Union's first assault gun armed with a 122 mm (4.8 in) howitzer. It had a speed of 55 km/h (34 mph), a combat weight of 34 tons, and carried five-man crew. It was similar in shape to the German StuG III. The SU-122 first saw action in the Battle of Kursk, took part in the recapture of Oryol and in the subsequent pursuit. It is finished in Dark Green. (Illustration by Dimitris Hadoulas/ Historical Notes by Stelios Demiras)

**SOVIET INFANTRYMAN, 40th SOVIET ARMY,
VORONEZH FRONT, KURSK 1943**
He wears the 1943 pattern *gimnastyorka* (shirt-tunic) in khaki color with
stand up collar and shoulder boards, *sharovary* (trousers) in same color
with "semi-breeches" in diamond shape with reinforcing patch at the
knee. Black leather boots. The steel helmet M1940 replaced the older
one M1936 type. He carries the *veshchevoi meshok* (back pack), the
plashch-palatka (rain cape/shelter half) and an entrenching tool. He
sports the Stalingrad medal. He is armed with a 7.62 mm
Mosin-Nagant 1891/30 rifle. The *Vintovka* (rifle) *Obrazets* (model)
sometimes called the 1891/30g is one of a series of rifles based on the
Mosin-Nagant Model 1891 that were the standard
rifles of the Russian Army until 1945. The
name Mosin-Nagant was from the designers;
the Belgian Nagant brothers with the
modifications by Colonel S.I. Mosin of
the Imperial Russian Army.
(Illustration by Johnny Shumate/
Historical Notes-Comments by
Stelios Demiras)

German Forces at the Battle of Kursk - July 1943

At the beginning of July 1943, 900,000 German troops, supported by 2,600 tanks and self-propelled guns, launched an attack on the Kursk Salient that was defended by 1,400,000 Soviets supported by 5,350 tanks. The Germans' insufficient assault infantry would decisively the outcome of this crucial battle.

Between 22 June 1941 and 1 July 1943, *Wehrmacht* losses on all fronts were a reported 3,950,000 dead, wounded, and missing-in-action. The majority of these casualties were the result of operations on the Eastern Front. By the beginning of July 1943, on average, each of the 243 German infantry divisions was under-strength by 2,500 personnel, according to the established organization tables.

German Panzer Major Franz Bäke, holder of the Knights' Cross of the Iron Cross, commanded the 2nd Battalion, 11th Panzer Regiment.

German Panther tank shortly before the Battle of Kursk.

The Stalingrad defeat during the winter of 1943 had resulted in the loss of 13 infantry, one mountain, three panzer and three mechanized divisions. In addition, three infantry and three panzer divisions lost on the North African front have to be added to this total.

The German High Command calculated that it had a net shortage of 800,000 men and this had to be covered immediately. Hitler was forced to take the necessary measures to resolve this situation. On the 22nd January 1943 he gave the order to:
a) mobilize the 1925 class, numbering 400,000 men aged 18 years,
b) mobilize men with specialized skills working in industry, communications, transportation and the general civil sector, numbering 200,000, and
c) call to arms another 200,000 men, aged between 21 and 42 years.

The total of Germans serving in the Armed Forces (*Wehrmacht, Kriegsmarine,* and *Luftwaffe*) on 3 May 1943 amounted to 9,500,000 men. This number would be dramatically eroded during the remaining years of war. Additionally, around one million Russian volunteers, ex-prisoners of war, also served in the *Wehrmacht*. These were known as "Hiwis" by the Germans (an abbreviation of the German word *Hilfswilliger*, meaning volunteer auxiliaries). Each German infantry division included at least 1,000 Hiwis. Another 900,000 Russians were working in Germany in the war industry and as farm labor.

By the beginning of 1943, also fighting alongside the Germans, were 176 anti-communist volunteer battalions from Georgia, Turkistan, Armenia, Chechnya, Azerbaijan and the northern Caucasus. These volunteers totaled around 320,000 men in June 1943.

The Germans had also mobilized ethnic Germans (*Volksdeutsche*) residing outside the Reich in the occupied countries. A grand total of 15,500,000 men and 14,800,000 women were working in the war industry and the civil sector, while 6,300,000 foreigners from all over Europe, either forcibly conscripted or as volunteers, were working in Germany in the war industry and in agriculture.

German *Sturmgeschutz mit* 8.8 cm Pak 43/2 (SdKfz 184) Ferdinand heavy assault gun/tank destroyer, '612', 654th Schwere Panzerjäger-Abteilung, Kursk, July 1943. Ferdinands were issued to 653 and 654 Schwere Panzerjäger-Abteilung in April and May 1943 and fought at the Battle of Kursk. The heavy metal "monster" of 65 tons was armed with the 8.8cm Pak 43/2 gun but lacking a machine gun for self defense was an easy task for the Soviet Infantry. As a long-range tank destroyer the Ferdinand achieved success, but at the Battle of Kursk was a failure. This Ferdinand is finished in a two-color camouflage scheme with Sand Yellow as the base color and irregularly shaped lines of Dark Green. (Illustration by Dimitris Hadoulas/Historical Notes by Stelios Demiras)

Forming new infantry Divisions

Following Hitler's diktat, by February 1943, 20 new infantry divisions had been formed, with sixteen in France, and one each in Germany, Denmark, the Balkans, and Russia. The number of battalions comprising each division was reduced from nine to six, and the total of men from 17,700 to 12,700. On the other hand, the number of machine guns and submachine guns in each battalion increased. It had been noted, though, that more than ever the infantry divisions required tank support to accomplish their missions. Only eight of these 20 new infantry divisions were sent to the Eastern Front. The others were assigned to Italy to await the expected Allied landings there. Furthermore, at the start of 1943, four existing infantry divisions were converted to mechanized ones.

Panzer Divisions Composition

Between January and March 1943, the German Army had lost 2,311 tanks on the Eastern Front. As of the end of March 1943, Germany had on the Eastern Front 902 operational tanks,

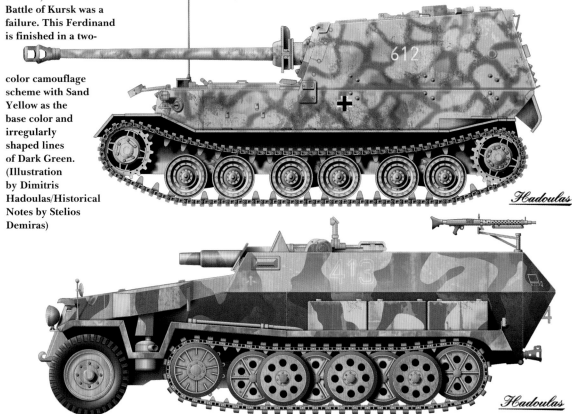

German *Mittlere Schutzenpanzerwagen 7.5cm (SdKfz 251/9) Ausf C* semi-tracked medium armored personnel carrier, 9./*Panzergrenadier-Regiment* 59, 20th Panzer Division, Kursk 1943. It had a combat weight of 8.53 tons, a speed of 53km/h, and carried a three-man crew. It was armed with a 7.5cm KwK37 (L/24) gun and two 7.92mm MG 34 or MG 42 machine guns. Designed to provide more flexible support for the Heavy Armor Infantry Company (Sp). It is finished in a two-color camouflage scheme with Sand Yellow as the basic color and irregular stripes in Olive Green. (Illustration by Dimitris Hadoulas/Historical Notes by Stelios Demiras)

**SS-UNTERSTURMFÜHRER
(2ND LIEUTENANT), DAS REICH
DIVISION, KURSK 1943**
He wears the five other Rank's standard jacket issue to the SS with pointed pocket flaps and peaked cap in field gray, 6x10 binoculars, black leather boots, gray gloves (suede), shirt and tie. He sports a Winter Campaign Medal 1941-42 button-hole ribbon. On his left sleeve is seen the cuff title *Das Reich*. He is armed with a Walter Pistol P38. As "A remarkably robust weapon, the P38 performed very well in the extreme cold of the Russian Front." It was accurate and easy to shoot well and was very popular for its effectiveness. (Illustration by Johnny Shumate / Historical Notes-Comments by Stelios Demiras)

German *Sturmpanzer Brummbär*, armed with a 15cm howitzer. Sixty-six of these were available during the Battle of Kursk.

784 tanks under repair, and 275 as strategic reserves. A total of 591 tanks had been damaged beyond recovery on the battlefields. Between April and June of that year, the Germans took delivery of 1,257 new tanks, but this still left them with a shortage of over 1,000 tanks on the Eastern Front.

A German panzer division in mid-1942 fielded 15,200 men equipped with 100 - 150 tanks. On 15 March 1943, the Army High Command (*Oberkommando des Heeres - OKH*) laid down a table of organization, in which it restricted the number of tanks in a division to a mere 85. The organic composition of a panzer division consisted of a regimental headquarters company with seven Panzer II, one Panzer I, and two Panzer III vehicles; a battalion headquarters company, organized like the regiment's, with three light tank companies with a total of 51 tanks; and one medium tank company with 14 tanks.

The German General Staff (*Grosser Generalstab*) issued a statement in June 1943 mentioning, among other things: "We hope that by December 1943, each panzer division will be equipped exclusively with Panzer IVs and

Panzer IIIs with the long 50mm gun and Panther tanks." This meant that, in July 1943, many older types of German tank were going to become prey to the Soviet T-34s at the Battle of Kursk.

The Germans still possessed the PzKpfw III tank in large numbers, armed either with the short 50mm KwK 39 L/42, the long 50mm L/60, or the short 75mm KwK L/24 gun, but the vehicle had proved ineffective against the Soviet T-34 and KV tanks. Attempts to up-gun the PzKpfw III's more advanced J and K versions with the long 50mm KwK L/60 gun were unsuccessful. The Panzer III tank equipped the panzer divisions with its mission being infantry support. The German Army's main battle tank remained the PzKpfw IV, and its "H" variant was armed with the long 75mm L/48 gun that was a relatively successful match for any Allied tank. On the other hand, the heavy PzKpfw VI Tiger I tank, armed with the deadly 88mm gun, could destroy any tank from a distance of two kilometers. It was an expensive weapon, however, both in terms of its high production costs and its greedy consumption of fuel. It was a tank that could ideally be used to fire against the enemy from pre-prepared positions, indeed a defensive tank par excellence. On 1 July 1943, there were 240 Tigers available on the Eastern Front, but only 178 of them were used during the Battle of Kursk.

Hitler had placed high hopes on the new PzKpfw V Panther tank, which had armor up to 100mm thick, high speed, and was armed with the excellent 75mm KwK 42 L/70 gun. Two hundred of these tanks were made available for the Kursk front but, in June 1943, the Inspector-General of Panzer Troops, General Heinz Guderian, reported to Hitler that problems with its transmission system and the inadequate engine cooling, leading to severe overheating, caused 65 of these tanks to be withdrawn for repair. Around 190 Panther tanks were used in the decisive Battle of Kursk, but many were immobilized because of mechanical breakdowns.

At the Battle of Kursk, the Germans fielded 1,865 modern tanks, 384 older tanks, 533 *Sturmgeschütz* assault guns, and 200 tank destroyers: a grand total of 2,982 armored fighting vehicles (AFVs) (including the ones under repair). One hundred flame-thrower tanks, all built on the Panzer III chassis, should be added to this total. The majority of these (28) were fielded by the élite Panzer Grenadier Division *Grossdeutschland* (*Panzergrenadier-Division*), with the remainder being distributed among the other panzer divisions.

Confronting the Germans at the Battle of Kursk were the Soviets' 5,350 tanks, of which 3,475 were T-34 Model 1942s or 1943s. In addition, KV-1 heavy tanks and a small number of T-26s were also present.

The SS Panzer Divisions Reorganization

In October 1942, each panzer regiment of the SS panzer grenadier divisions was composed as follows: a regimental headquarters company, an engineer company, a panzer battalion headquarters company, two light panzer companies, one medium panzer company, and a maintenance and supply company. Then, in November of the same year, the three SS divisions, 1st *Leibstandarte Adolf Hitler,* 2nd *Das Reich,* and the 3rd *Totenkopf* were converted to panzer grenadier divisions. Later, on 1 May 1943, the *Leibstandarte* Division was reinforced with a panzer battalion, consisting of four medium panzer companies and a heavy panzer company equipped with 15 Tigers. The *Das Reich* Division acquired a panzer battalion, with two light panzer and two medium panzer companies, a panzer battalion of one light panzer company and one company equipped with ex-Soviet T-34 tanks, as well as a

German fuel train in Russia. Re-supply of the German forces greatly improved during 1943.

German *Panzerjäger 38(t) für 7.62cm PaK36 (r) (SdKfz 139)* or *Marder III* self-propelled captured anti-tank gun on tank chassis , 92nd *Panzerjäger-Abteilung*, 20th Panzer Division, Kursk 1943. It was armed with a 7.62cm PaK36 (r) L/51.5 gun and one 7.92mm MG 37(t) machine gun. It had a combat weight of 10.67 tons, a speed of 42km/h, and carried a four-man crew. Total production

company of 15 Tigers. Finally, the *Totenkopf* Division had two panzer battalions, with a total of two light panzer and four medium panzer companies, and a heavy panzer company also equipped with 15 Tigers. The SS divisions' panzer regiments were recalled to Germany, to be familiarized and equipped with the new Panther tanks.

Independent Armored Units

The German Staff decided not to have the Panther tank units organic to the panzer divisions, but to organize them as independent units. The first such unit to be formed in January 1943 was the 51st Panzer Battalion (*Panzer-Abteilung*). It consisted of one

of the Marder III was 344 (from April to October 1942) plus 19 converted from PzKpfw 38(t) in 1943. It is finished in a two-color camouflage scheme with Sand Yellow as the basic color and irregular shaped stripes in Olive Green or Dark Green. (Illustration by Dimitris Hadoulas/Historical Notes by Stelios Demiras)

German *Panzerkampfwagen III Ausf N*, 3rd Panzer Regiment, 2nd Panzer Division, Kursk 1943. The *Pz III Ausf N* was similar to the J, L, and M types. The major difference being that its gun was replaced with the 5cm weapon of the previous versions. The new KwK L/24 7.5cm gun was more effective against enemy tanks and, very soon, the new Pz III became a tank crew favorite. It had a combat weight of 23 tons, a speed of 40 km/h, and carried a five-man crew. There were 155 *Pz III Ausf Ns* available during the Battle of Kursk in the panzer forces of Army Groups Center and South. This tank is finished in a two-color scheme with Sand Yellow as the base color and irregularly shaped, over-painted patches of Dark Green. The three-digit tank code was only painted on the rear of the turret. (Illustration by Dimitris Hadoulas/ Historical Notes by Stelios Demiras)

**UNTEROFFIZIER (NCO),
KURSK 1943**
Of special note are the *Heer* (Army)
Splinter Pattern Smock and *Heer
Splinter* Helmet Cover of the M1942
type. He wears the standard-issue field
gray service dress (M 40 tunic and
trousers) and M1939 Jackboots
(marching boots). He is armed with an
MP 40 machine pistol with two triple
canvas magazine pouches.
He carries a *splinter Zeltbahn*,
breadbag, canteen, mess tin,
entrenching tool with
bayonet M1898 and stick
grenades M1929.
(Illustration by Johnny
Shumate/ Historical
Notes-Comments by
Stelios Demiras)

panzer battalion headquarters company (with eight Panther tanks) and four companies with 22 Panthers each. Each of these independent units had a total of 96 tanks. The 52nd Panzer Battalion was formed in February 1943 with Panther tanks. Both these units took part in the Battle of Kursk.

Many historical analysts have been critical of the German command for forming independent units equipped with Panther tanks, seeing the move as depriving the German panzer divisions of extra firepower. From the beginning of 1944, all Panther panzer units became organic to the panzer divisions. It is believed however that, given that this new tank encountered many technical and mechanical problems on the battlefield, incorporating the independent Panther tank units organically into the panzer divisions would not have altered the final outcome of the Battle of Kursk.

It had been planned that, in January 1943, each German panzer division would be provided a heavy panzer company equipped with the Tiger tank, but the heavy panzer battalions (other than those belonging to the SS) actually operated independently. The table of equipment for a heavy panzer battalion included 45 Tigers and 45 Panzer IIIs. Only the elite *Grossdeutschland* Division fielded a fully-equipped Tiger heavy panzer battalion.

It was also decided, in January 1943, to reinforce each panzer division with a self-propelled assault gun battalion (*Sturmgeschütz-Abteilung*). By the time of the battle, however, only the 14th, 16th, and 24th Panzer Divisions were equipped with an assault gun battalion, each consisting of four batteries with a total of three

Panzer III command tanks and 93 *Sturmgeschütz* IIIs.

Another independent unit that participated in the Battle of Kursk was the 216th Assault Gun Battalion, equipped with 45 *Sturmpanzer* IV *Brummbär* assault guns, which were armed with 150mm howitzers and given the task of destroying enemy fortified positions. Other independent assault gun units employed during the battle were equipped with a total of 533 *Sturmgeschütz* IIIs.

Additionally, the 653rd and 654th Heavy Anti-tank Battalions (*Schwere Panzerjäger-Abteilung*) were used as independent units. These were equipped with 90 *Ferdinand* self-propelled anti-tank guns, which were incredibly massive pieces of equipment and were armed with the deadly 88mm gun. Their mission was to break through the Soviet defensive zones and to destroy any obstacle they met. Finally, around 200 self-propelled anti-tank guns, mainly of the Marder type, were employed in independent units.

The German Order of Battle at the Battle of Kursk

The German pincer movement that would trap the Soviet forces in the Kursk Salient consisted of the 2nd and 9th Armies and the 4th Panzer Army (*Panzerarmee*) and the Army Detachment Kempf (*Armeeabteilung*). In particular, the 9th Army, under the eminently capable General Walter Model, would be the northern part of the pincer and would launch from the Oryol area. The 9th Army was assigned to Army Group Center (*Heeresgruppe Mitte*), commanded by Field Marshal Hans Günther von Kluge. The 2nd Army, under General

Rudolf Schmidt, would cover the 9th Army's flank and would prevent a Soviet strike on the western face of the salient. The 4th Panzer Army, under General Hermann Hoth, would be the southern end of the pincer and would cooperate with Army Detachment Kempf (named after its commanding officer, General Werner Kempf) that would reinforce the 4th Panzer Army's attack plan. These forces were part of Army Group South, commanded by Field Marshal Erich von Manstein, probably the most talented German general of the war, and would launch its attack from the area of Khar'kov in a northerly direction. Finally, the 1st Air Division (*Flieger-Division*), under Major General Paul Deichmann and assigned to the 6th Air Fleet (*Luftflotte*), and the 4th Air Fleet would support the ground forces with 2,000 aircraft.

9th Army Composition

The 9th Army fielded:
● XXIII (23rd) Corps (*Armeekorps,*) under General Johannes Friessner,

with the 338th Infantry Division (*Infanterie-Division*, nine battalions), the 216th Infantry Division (six battalions) and the 78th Assault Division (*Sturm-Division*, six battalions, two anti-tank battalions - *Panzerjäger-Abteilung*- and one self-propelled assault gun battalion equipped with *Sturmgeschütz*). Also attached to this corps was the 87th Infantry Regiment (*Infanterie-Regiment*, 36th Infantry Division).
● XLI (41st) Panzer Corps, General of Panzer Troops Josef Harpe, with the 86th Infantry Division (six battalions), the 292nd Infantry Division (six battalions), and the 18th Panzer Division (with 75 tanks, only 32 of which were modern types, and this number also included those under repair). Attached were: the 656th Anti-tank Regiment (*Panzerjäger-Regiment*, with 90 Ferdinand self-propelled anti-tank guns), the 216th Assault Gun Battalion (with 66 *Sturmpanzer IV Brummbär* assault guns), two *Sturmgeschütz* assault gun battalions, and two anti-tank battalions.
● XLVII (47th) Panzer Corps, General of Panzer Troops Joachim

German Panzer IV Ausf. H, armed with a 7.5cm gun and side skirts as protection against Soviet light anti-tank weapons.

German 15cm *Schweres Infanteriegeschütz 33 (Sf) auf Panzerkampfwagen 38 (t) Ausf H (SdKfz 138/1)* or *Grille* self-propelled heavy infantry gun on tank chassis, 12th Panzergrenadier Regiment, 4th Panzer Division, Kursk 1943. It was armed with a 15cm sIG33/1 gun and one 7.92mm MG 34. It had a combat weight of 11.5 tons, a speed of 35km/h, and carried a five-man crew. Total production of SdKfz 138/1 (Grille) was 90 (from February to April 1943) plus one prototype. It is finished in a two-color camouflage scheme with Sand Yellow as the basic color and irregular shaped patches of Olive Green. (Illustration by Dimitris Hadoulas/ Historical Notes by Stelios Demiras)

Hermann August Lemelsen, with the 6th Infantry Division (nine battalions), the 20th Panzer Division (85 tanks, 60 of these being modern types), the 9th Panzer Division (111 tanks, 64 of these being modern types), and the 2nd Panzer Division (136 tanks, 40 Panthers). Attached were: the 505th Heavy Tank Battalion (*Schwere Panzerabteilung*; 25 Panzer IIIs and 20 Tigers), and two *Sturmgeschütz* assault gun battalions.

● XLVI (46th) Panzer Corps, General of Infantry Hans Zorn. This corps, although titled "panzer," consisted of infantry divisions: the 31st Infantry Division (six battalions), although this division was totally exhausted following the battles for the Rzhev salient, the 7th Infantry Division (nine battalions), the 258th Infantry Division (seven battalions), the 102nd Infantry Division (six battalions), and three self-propelled anti-tank battalions.

● XX (20th) Corps, General Rudolf Freiherr von Roman, with the 72nd

Infantry Division (six battalions), the 45th Infantry Division (six battalions – a division that had been badly mauled in the January/February 1943 battles), the 137th Infantry Division (six battalions), and the 251st Infantry Division – a battle-ready division at full strength of nine battalions.

9th Army reserves were the 36th Infantry Division, the 4th Panzer Division (101 tanks, 79 of these being modern types), the 12th Panzer Division (68 tanks, 36 of these being modern types), and the 10th Panzer Grenadier Division.

2nd Army Composition

The 2nd Army's mission, under the command of General Rudolf Schmidt, was to cover the 9th Army's flank on the western face of the Kursk Salient. It comprised the 82nd Infantry Division, that had been badly mauled in the battles for the Kastornoye Salient, consisting of six battalions whose troops were mostly recruits, the 340th Infantry Division (six battalions), the 327th Infantry Division regiment, the 88th Infantry Division (nine battalions that was exhausted

SS-SCHÜTZE (PRIVATE), 1st SS
PANZER GRENADIER DIVISION
*LEIBSTANDARTE ADOLF HITLER
(LAH)*, II SS PANZER CORPS, 4th
PANZER ARMY, ARMY GROUP SOUTH,
KURSK 1943
He wears the standard-issue field gray service
dress (M40 tunic and trousers) and M1939
Jackboots (marching boots). Of special note are
the Waffen-SS M42 Helmet Cover, Type-I and
the SS Smock, Type II, Oak A. He is armed with
the multi-purpose MG 42 machine gun. He
carries the standard machine gunner's
equipment; the MG 42 toolbox, a P38 pistol in
its 'hard-shell' holster, M1939 leather infantry
support straps, SS enlisted man's belt, bread
bag, M1931 mess kit, entrenching tool and
bayonet M1898. The MG 42 was extremely
reliable, highly resistant to dust and cold
conditions, and was very popular in the
German Army. It was first used in action
by the Deutsches Afrikakorps at Ghazalah
in May 1942, and more than 750,000 MG
42 were made before the war ended.
(Illustration by Johnny Shumate /
Historical Notes-Comments
by Stelios Demiras)

after the fierce battles of the winter of 1943), and the 68th Infantry Division with its six battalions of inferior fighting capacity that had been assigned to the Army.

4th Panzer Army Composition

The 4th Panzer Army, under the experienced General of Panzer Troops Hermann Hoth, was the most powerful of the German forces and the southern part of the pincer. It would commence its attack from its positions between Komarovka and Belgorod, on the southern face of the salient, towards Kursk to the north. Its Order of Battle was as follows:

● LII (52nd) Corps, General of Infantry Eugen Ott, with the 57th Infantry Division (nine battalions) that had not fully recovered from the battles at the beginning of 1943, the 255th Infantry Division (six battalions), and the 332nd Infantry Division (nine battalions) that had been formed in France and had only reached Russia in March 1943.

● XLVIII (48th) Panzer Corps, commanded by General of Panzer Troops Otto von Knobelsdorff, was positioned on the flanks of LII Corps to the east. It fielded the Panzer Grenadier Division *Grossdeutschland,* an elite formation consisting of six infantry battalions and 136 tanks (104 of these being modern types), the 167th Infantry Division (a full-strength division with nine battalions), the 3rd Panzer Division (102 tanks, 63 of these being modern types), the 39th Panzer Regiment (*Panzer-Regiment*) with 200 Panther tanks, the 502nd Heavy Tank Battalion with four Panzer II and 14 Tiger tanks, and the 911th Assault Gun Battalion with 45 *Sturmgeschütz* IIIs.

● II (2nd) SS Panzer Corps, under the experienced Waffen-SS General

Paul Hausser, with three elite SS Panzer grenadier divisions: the 1st Panzer Grenadier Division *Leibstandarte Adolf Hitler* (117 tanks, 98 of these being modern types), to which was assigned an assault gun battalion equipped with 34 *Sturmgeschütz* IIIs, the 2nd Panzer Grenadier Division *Das Reich* (*SS-Panzer-Grenadier-Division Das Reich*) (163 tanks, 128 of these being modern types and 34 assault guns), and the 3rd Panzer Grenadier Division *Totenkopf* (148 tanks, 140 of these being modern types and 35 assault guns). All these formations were highly trained and consisted of young men with high morale.

Army Detachment Kempf Composition

The Army Detachment Kempf was positioned east of the II SS Panzer Corps and was commanded by General of Panzer Troops Werner Kempf. Its orders were to launch its attack from its positions in the Khar'kov area, advance towards Kursk, through Belgorod, while simultaneously covering the flanks of II SS Panzer Corps. Its subordinate corps were:

● III (3rd) Panzer Corps, General of Panzer Troops Hermann Breith. Its formations were the 6th Panzer Division that had reached the Eastern Front from France in December 1942 (124 tanks, 86 of these being modern types), the 168th Infantry Division (nine battalions) that was still recovering from the battles of January 1943, the 19th Panzer Division (90 tanks, 58 of these being modern types), and the 7th Panzer Division (112 tanks, 80 of these being modern types). The 228th Assault Gun Battalion (35 *Sturmgeschütz* III), and the 503rd Heavy Tank Battalion (48 Tiger tanks) were assigned to the corps.

● Raus XI (11th) Corps, General of Panzer Troops Erhard Raus, with the 106th and the 320th Infantry Divisions (nine battalions each). These formations had arrived at the front from France at the beginning of the year. This corps was supported by the 905th Assault Gun Battalion that was equipped with *Sturmgeschütz* IIIs.

● XLII (42nd) Corps, General of Infantry Franz Mattenklott, with the 282nd Infantry Division (nine battalions) that had arrived from France in March 1943, the 39th Infantry Division (nine battalions) that had also been formed in France but lacked combat experience, and the 161st Infantry Division (nine battalions) that had also been reorganized in France. Younger recruits as well as veterans made up this division that was possessed of high morale. Additionally, the corps was reinforced with two self-propelled anti-tank battalions equipped with the Hornisse that was armed with the 88mm gun. Its area of responsibility, 40km in length, was on the bend of the River Donets and its mission was to cover the flanks of Army Group Kempf. It was therefore not expected to participate actively in the operations.

Conclusions

When they launched their invasion of the Soviet Union – code named Operation "Barbarossa" – in June 1941, the Germans attacked with 1,320,000 men supported by 3,420 tanks along a 3,000km front. At the Battle of Kursk, they fielded 2,600 tanks and 900,000 men along a front of just 120km, so they had good reason to be optimistic about the outcome of the operation. The Soviets' superiority in the number of their tanks did not particularly cause concern among the German Staff, who trusted in the superior training of the German tank crews, as well as in the spirit of initiative and improvisation that they were free to use during the battle. The 20 infantry divisions that had been destroyed at Stalingrad had been reformed but, instead of being used at Kursk, they were then transferred to continental Italy and Sicily, where an Allied landing was expected. In retrospect, these divisions could have been of vital importance for a successful outcome of the operation at Kursk, especially on the northern face of the Salient (a sector under General Model), if the course and outcome of the Battle of Kursk in July 1943 is to be judged by hindsight.

Ferdinand tank destroyer, fitted with an 8.8cm gun. Hitler had high hopes for these mechanical "beasts," but the end results during the Battle of Kursk were very disappointing due, mainly, to technical unreliability.

The Soviet Defensive Zone Around the Kursk Salient

Taking into consideration the expected German attack, the gigantic defense network that the Soviets had methodically built around Kursk was carefully planned and equipped with the necessary means to fulfill one particular function: to constitute the main element in checking and weakening the armored might of the *Wehrmacht*. Historians have characterized the confrontation at Kursk as a modern repetition of trench warfare. Some of the cheapest weapons, such as the grenade, the anti-tank rifle, the Molotov cocktail, indeed all types of explosives and especially the mines, were the primary weapons of the defenders and attackers in this attritional clash without par.

These Panzergrenadiers carry on their way on foot, after passing through a burning Russian village. In the foreground the Panzergrenadier is wearing a camouflaged tunic.

The Soviet High Command had been expecting a German attack on the Kursk Salient since its recapture on 8 February, and especially following the stabilization of the front during the fierce battles of March 1943. Manstein eagerly planned for an immediate new operation without delay, with Kursk as its objective, after the recapture of Khar'kov on 15 March and Belgorod on 18 March. The German successes had created a bulge 180km wide and 120km deep with the historical town of Kursk at its center. In the meantime, the Soviets were busy collecting intelligence about German intentions. The nature of the bulge was an extremely attractive objective, while both camps knew that the epicenter of any operation would be in the southern sector of the front. Field Marshal Georgy Konstantinovich Zhukov (promoted to that rank in January) submitted a detailed memorandum to Stalin on which to base the strategy of a decisive

**SOVIET TANK BUSTER, INFANTRY REGIMENT,
48th ARMY, KURSK 1943**
He wears the 1943 pattern *gymnastiorka* (shirt-tunic) with stand up
collar and shoulder boards in khaki color, *sharovari* (trousers) in
same color with "semi-breeches" with diamond shape and
reinforcing patch at the knee. Raspberry piping on shoulder boards
for infantry. The steel helmet M1940 replaced the older one M1936
type. He carries the *veshchevoi meshok* (back pack) and the *plashch-
palatka* (rain cape/shelter half). He is armed with the PTRD-41
14.5mm anti-tank rifle with PTRD-41 20-round cartridge pouch.
(Illustration by Johnny Shumate / Historical Notes-Comments by
Stelios Demiras)

Soldiers from 6th Panzer Division are investing a Russian village which has recently been subjected to an artillery barrage.

confrontation with the opponent. The Red Army would not attempt to launch another attack, but would instead challenge the *Wehrmacht* to undertake the offensive initiative. Intelligence gathered from extensive air reconnaissance, in conjunction with partisan activity, pointed to an imminent German operation on the Kursk front. In accordance with Zhukov's strategy, it was planned initially to have the Red Army act in defense in order to wear down the attacking enemy panzer divisions. Then, it would mount a counteroffensive with the objective of destroying any forces remaining. Zhukov had faith in the concept of defense-in-depth; an idea that had proved its value during the Battle of Moscow. He correctly assumed that, especially after the heavy mauling the Germans had suffered at Stalingrad, the defeat of the *Wehrmacht* would depend on drawing it into a well-prepared trap that would engulf its infantry, and, more importantly, its mechanized and armored forces. If this proved successful, it would remove any strategic initiative from the German staff and would ultimately lead to a complete and irrevocable reversal of

the balance on the Eastern Front in favor of the Soviets.

The Allies were strengthening the USSR with all kinds of war matériel, and production from Soviet defense industries was improving, allowing the deployment of new weaponry on the battlefield. It was becoming clear which side this new balance of power would favor. The Kursk Salient was believed to be the ideal operational environment for the fulfillment of the Soviet plans. The terrain worked in favor of the defender because many rivers crossed the area and there was a lack of any road network. While great rivers and rushing torrents traversed the area, it was also ravaged during the summer by sudden, torrential downpours. Many small villages and provincial towns offered abundant cover for the defending forces. Four rivers divided the area into several sectors. The Seym and Svapa Rivers in the center and north respectively divided the salient in two, providing a natural obstacle that could easily impede a large-scale attack from the west towards Kursk. In the south, the Psyol and Donets Rivers formed another natural obstacle, preventing the enemy from closely approaching to the southeast of Kursk. In general, all

Many tanks were put out of action due to the accuracy of Russian anti-tank fire during the German attack on the Soviet defense zones that secured the approaches to Kursk. This Panther was hit in the engine compartment and subsequently destroyed by the ensuing fire. Note the recovery cable that shows an attempt was made to recover it from the battlefield.

these rivers favored the defense as they channeled any attacking force into specific, easily predictable avenues of approach that could easily be fortified and defended. Between the main rivers, there were also many smaller rivers and streams which, throughout the operations, formed additional obstacles, swollen as they were by the summer rains. Many small rural towns could be fortified and so become part of the integrated defense zone restricting the movement of mechanized formations. In order to advance, the attacker would be forced to clear all farming hamlets to cover his rear and flanks, wasting both time and forces in the process. In addition, field observation favored the defender, while fields of fire were generally very good. The terrain was open farmland with fields of wheat, and sparse groups of trees that did not offer enough cover to the attacker. This general lack of cover favored the defending forces by allowing observation in depth, thus removing any element of surprise. The terrain gave a well-prepared defender the opportunity to strike at the enemy in many sectors, while remaining virtually invisible, something the Germans were going to experience to their bitter cost. There already existed

trenches and other fortifications in the area from the previous battles.

Stalin gave his consent to the strategy of drawing the Germans into a battle of attrition and, on 12 April, following a major conference with the *Stavka* (General Headquarters), gave the orders for the fortification of the salient and its transformation into a huge "anti-tank fortress."

Thanks to their secret agent, code-named "Lucy," the Soviets were also aware of many details of German intentions, which helped them to avoid both a strategic or tactical surprise. In addition, the British intelligence service, which was in possession of the German "Enigma" decrypting machine and its "Ultra" codes, had deciphered messages concerning the movements of units on the Eastern Front that revealed the German intention of mounting an assault in the Kursk area.

German plans were initially assessed by an outstanding staff officer, Nikolay Fyodorovich Vatutin, Commander-in-Chief of the Voronezh Front from March 1943, who showed amazing foresight in predicting the operation's final form. Vatutin estimated that, because of the terrain characteristics, the German attack could be launched from just two

The Soviet 14.5mm PTRS 1941 semi-automatic anti-tank rifle was a Red Army weapon that was little used, much like its cousin, the PTRD 1941, because it was quite complicated and often jammed. It held a five-round, hollow-charge magazine, was 2.108m long, over all, and could penetrate 25mm armor at a range of 500 m. (Illustration by Dimitris Hadoulas/ Historical Notes by Stelios Demiras)

directions. Army Group Center could only cover the shorter distance and bypass the obstacles of the Seym and Svapa Rivers, using the Oryol - Kursk railroad line, by launching its attack from the north in the direction of Kursk. Army Group South, in the south, could only penetrate towards Prokhorovka, a key town and the only accessible area between the Psyol and Donets Rivers. This avenue of attack was the most suitable for an advance towards Kursk because it bypassed the Psyol River and would allow the *Wehrmacht* formations to approach their objectives without having to bridge the river obstacles under enemy fire. The German and Soviet staffs knew that the towns of Kursk and Prokhorovka were of special importance in the salient. Prokhorovka, in particular, was a large town and an important defense, transportation, and supply hub for the Soviets and it was connected by railroad to Kursk. The town of Kursk dominated the center of the salient, being the main road and railway hub in the region. Its capture would, automatically, lead to the encirclement of the large concentration of Soviet forces in the salient and, additionally, it would give a great boost for the further carrying out of operations. It was the perfect bait to challenge the enemy to attack there, although the Soviets had to find enough time to prepare its defense by taking advantage of every day that the attack did not materialize to build up its defending forces and fortifying the area.

Organizing the Defensive Network

Following *Stavka* orders, Field Marshals Zhukov and Aleksandr Mikhaylovich Vasilevsky went to Kursk at the end of April to organize its defense. Construction of fortification works began immediately. The Soviets knew that it was a race between the two armies, each of which feverishly set about reinforcing its positions with the most troops and all possible means to try to attain superiority over the opponent. In this race, time favored the defender. Priority was given to restoring the strength and reinforcing those forces already in the area. For example, the 6th Guards Army (formerly the 21st Army, the honorary title having been awarded in February 1943, following the Battle of Stalingrad) that moved to the Kursk area was under-strength in both men and matériel. The USSR had a vast manpower pool from which to draw its conscripts. Despite the huge losses sustained during the first six months of 1943, the Red Army increased its strength by a million men. From 1 January to 15 July 1943, 2,875,000 men were sent to the front. Fifty-seven per cent of them reinforced the five fronts that participated in operations against "Zitadelle." Between April and June 1943, the strength of the infantry divisions in the Kursk salient reached levels of 8,000-9,000 troops (Soviet regulations stipulated a strength of 9,534 men for an infantry division and

9,680 for a Guards infantry division). The two Fronts already positioned in the salient, the Central and Voronezh, had priority for any reinforcements. During March, the 1st Tank Army was sent to reinforce the Voronezh Front. These two fronts were further reinforced between April and June as follows:

a) Central Front: eight infantry divisions, three anti-tank brigades, two independent anti-tank regiments, three artillery brigades, eight artillery regiments, two armored brigades and two independent armored regiments.

b) Voronezh Front: six infantry divisions, two anti-tank brigades, 22 independent anti-tank regiments, eight artillery regiments, two mortar brigades, three Guards mortar brigades (the Guards mortar formations were equipped with the *Katyusha* multiple rocket launchers), ten armored brigades and five independent armored regiments. As can be seen, the majority of the forces were sent to the southern sector of the front, reinforcing Vatutin's forces. While it is true that the Soviets fielded a larger number of tanks than the Germans, one third of them were light types, such as the BT, T-60, and T-70, which were used for reconnaissance and infantry support. A great number were T-34/76s, while the new self-propelled SU-76 and SU-152 guns were also represented. The fortuitous capture of a Tiger tank in the Leningrad area in November 1942 had prematurely revealed its secrets. Both tank and the anti-tank gun crews were

under strict orders and were trained hard and methodically on the best way to hit the Tiger's vulnerable points. The artillery arm was reinforced in unprecedented numbers so that for every two infantry regiments, there was an artillery regiment. Weaponry was extensively and radically modernized. The outmoded organizational table for a tank destroyer division, composed of mixed artillery regiments equipped with 76mm, 45mm, and 37mm guns, had proved inadequate. Anti-tank brigades of two regiments equipped with 76mm guns and one 57mm or 45mm gun regiment, were now formed. With the revised organizational table, each brigade commander had between 60 and 72 anti-tank guns under his control. Twenty-seven anti-tank brigades (81 regiments) had been formed by 1 July with most of these formations taking part in the Kursk battles. Additionally, independent anti-tank regiments, equipped with 20 to 24 guns of 76mm or 45mm caliber, were formed. These units were assigned to the reserves of either an army or a particular front. At the same time, 35 independent anti-tank battalions were equipped with 85mm guns and became organic to the tank and mechanized corps. The battalions towed anti-tank artillery units, using US-built two-ton Dodge trucks that that gave them high mobility and the ability to move quickly to any area that required fire support. Soviet doctrine did not share the view that the best anti-tank weapon was the tank itself.

Soviet 14.5mm PTRD 1941 anti-tank rifle. One of the Red Army's most common anti-tank rifles. It weighed 17.3kg, had an overall length of 2.02m, and could penetrate 25mm of armor at a range of 500m. It fired hollow-charge rounds. It was also used by the partisans and the German forces. (Illustration by Dimitris Hadoulas/ Historical Notes by Stelios Demiras)

On the contrary, the Soviets believed that large concentrations of artillery (howitzers and anti-tank guns) were capable of stopping a panzer assault in its tracks and claimed that 60 anti-tank guns could successfully face a German panzer division. Large numbers of guns were positioned to cover those areas where the main *Wehrmacht* attack was expected to begin. For example, the concentration of howitzers and mortars was 91.6 per kilometer (an average of 85 barrels per kilometer) in the 13th Army defensive line in the northern sector, while anti-tank gun concentration was 23.7 per kilometer. By comparison, during the Battle of Moscow the concentration of howitzers and mortars was a mere 7 to 11 per kilometer, and during the Battle of Stalingrad it was 13.4 per kilometer.

Meanwhile, the partisans were mobilized and ordered to carry out the maximum possible sabotage to the enemy's infrastructure. In consequence, in the months up to July 1943, over 1,000 attacks on the rail network between Germany and the Eastern Front were reported.

Special attention was placed on employing deception (*Maskirovka*). Minefields, command and observation posts, artillery, and anti-tank positions were camouflaged with a high degree of success. The Soviets also extensively camouflaged the fortified positions while, at the same time, creating dummy ones. Over 1,000km of dummy trenches were dug to deceive the German reconnaissance aircraft. More than 900 dummy tanks formed a non-existent force, while 13 dummy airfields were built. The concealment of the actual size of their forces in the operational area was especially effective. So successful were the Soviets at deception that the Germans estimated that they had fielded strong armored forces on the east of the salient but were ignorant as to their size and strength or as to when they could reinforce the defenses in Kursk. Zhukov's orders were clear. The enemy must not realize the actual extent of the defensive preparations. A strict order was issued for the troops to move only at night and it was forbidden to mention these moves over the radio. Coordination between commanders was done in person, i.e., face-to-face, without the use of any other means of communication. The troops trained constantly and the postponement of the German attack gave them yet more time to do so. New manuals and regulations were compiled, taking into account all the lessons and experience gained from the bloody operations of the preceding years. The leadership ordered all formations and units to conduct a series of exercises to the letter and in total secrecy, within a framework of carefully planned training schedules. Even units on the front's first echelon began gradually, in a rolling schedule, to retire to the rear, so that all units without exception completed the arduous training program. First line units (first and second echelon) focused their training more on intercepting the German panzers. Everyone, from the commanding officer to the lowest private, was aware that the basic goal of all this intensive preparation was to stop the panzers' advance at all costs. Each man had memorized the Tiger's vulnerable points. Exercises in many forms were conducted and questions were put, such as: "...if the enemy attacks this point in this strength, how should we react and what plan should we follow?"

The defensive planning, combined within the overall plans of the Soviet leadership, fully satisfied one of the basic principles of war, "Concentrate the fighting strength at the decisive place on the battlefield at the appropriate time." This principle became the foundation on which the defense network around Kursk was established. While it is axiomatic that a superiority of 3 to 1 is the minimum for the attacker mounting an assault operation to have prospects of success, during the Kursk operations, the Soviets had 1.9 to 1 superiority in tanks, 2.5 to 1 in troops and 2.1 to 1 in guns. When "Zitadelle" started, nothing favored the attacker.

The Soviets developed a complex defensive system, consisting of an extensive trench network and fortified positions with intermediate dug-in positions for tanks, supported by thousands of weapons (howitzers, guns, mortars, rockets) positioned in prearranged firing positions, covering all possible avenues of approach. Eight defensive lines were constructed with Kursk as their hub and thousands of mines were laid between the lines. The Army units of the first defense echelon were deployed in the first three defensive lines. The first two comprised the tactical defense zone, with a total depth of 20km. The first of these two lines was the main defense line and was manned by the first echelon divisions. Fifteen kilometers behind it was the second defense line, where units of the infantry corps' second echelon were positioned. The third defense line, called the army rear line, was covered by the reserve units of the armies fighting in the first line (first-echelon armies). In the event that the enemy penetrated the first two lines, the defenders would fall back to the third, where, with the help of the reserves, they would drive back the invaders, in accordance with pre-planned strategy. A further three lines, manned by the front's reserve units, were constructed behind the first three primary defense lines. If the attacker succeeded in also penetrating these, he would reach the Steppe Front defense line, dominating the "neck" of the

During the Operation "Zitadelle" the Germany destroyed 1,600 Russian tanks (or assault tanks). The German forces between 5 July and 31 August 1943 lost 1,331 tanks.

salient. Finally, there was yet another defense line along the eastern banks of the Don River. This whole defensive system covered a depth of 250km.

In April 1943, *Stavka* issued instructions for the construction of fortified positions on the battlefield. The planning and construction of the defense lines around Kursk was based on this order. Its basis was the battalion defense area, which had a frontage of about 2km and a depth of 1.5 - 2km. This was further sub-divided into company and platoon strong points, where anti-tank guns were deployed. The divisional defense sectors were much narrower than they had been in previous battles (between 6 and 9km in each sector), thanks to the availability of a large number of troops. Frontages were even shorter where the enemy's main effort was expected, allowing a larger concentration of troops and means of support and more firepower coverage. The usual organization of the divisional defense sector, on the primary defense line, was based on the principle of "two units forward, one in reserve," that is, the deployment of two battalions from each of two regiments at the front. The third battalion of these regiments was positioned about 2km to the rear while the third regiment occupied a third line about 5km from the front. Each of these battalions deployed in a battalion defense area with prepared trenches and weapons emplacements.

The Soviets constructed a strong defensive zone from three lines of battalion defense areas. Each of these battalion defense areas consisted of two or three lines of trenches. The first trench line was protected by minefields and barbed wire and was defended by infantry, machine guns, and anti-tank weapons. Anti-tank rifles were positioned in the outposts to prevent a surprise penetration by enemy panzers. Anti-tank minefields were laid between the outposts and the first trench line. These were covered by machine-gun and rifle fire that prevented the enemy sappers from clearing them and opening lanes, and also by anti-tank guns that would be used against enemy panzers moving in lanes previously cleared. Heavy support weapons were positioned at a distance of between 200 and 1,000 meters, while the infantry was positioned as in the second and third trench lines. These weapons provided covering fire for the first line trenches and gave depth to the defensive position. Alternate positions were prepared that could be used to protect the regiment's flanks in the event of a breakthrough in a neighboring sector. The combat trenches were connected by communication trenches, in order that reinforcements and supplies could come forward and troops could be evacuated without being exposed to enemy fire. These could also be used by troops in the outposts to fall back in case of an enemy penetration.

At Kursk, each infantry corps deployed in two echelons, two infantry divisions in the first, with a third in the second echelon (a second division was also deployed in critical areas). The corps second echelon division, or divisions, manned the second defense line, which was located at a distance of 12 - 20km behind the main line of resistance. This particular distance was chosen in order to force the enemy to regroup his forces and reposition his artillery before making an assault on the next line. This would give the defenders extra time to evacuate their forces and re-organize in the next defense line. The second defense line was, in essence, organized like the first and was, similarly, protected by extensive minefields. In the majority of cases, however, the fortifications were

SOVIET ARMY SCOUT (*RAZVEDCHIK*), KURSK 1943
He wears a camouflage coverall (green and black patches) over standard uniform; the 1943 pattern *gimnastyorka* (shirt-tunic) in khaki color with stand up collar and shoulder boards, *sharovary* (trousers) in same color with "semi-breeches" in diamond shape with reinforcing patch at the knee. Black leather boots and *pilotka* (side cap). He is armed with a PPSh-41 7.62mm submachine gun with 71-round magazine. The machine pistol PPSh (*Pistolet Pulemyot Shpagina*) designed by Georgi Shpagin was developed in 1940-41 in an effort to design a weapon more suited to mass production than the PPD-40 model. This weapon came to be identified with the Russian soldier, as much as the MP 38 was for the German. The PPSh was rugged, simple, cheap, and effective. More than five million were made. (Illustration by Johnny Shumate / Historical Notes-Comments by Stelios Demiras)

not as extensive. The 7th Guards Army deployed three divisions in the first line and three in the second. The 6th Guards Army, manning the defense north and west of Belgorod, had four divisions in the first line and three in the second. The 13th Army, on the north face of the front, had four divisions in the first line and two in the second.

About 15km from the second line was a third defensive line (or the army rear defense line), which was organized like the first two and protected by minefields. Its purpose was to contain any penetration by enemy panzer spearheads, the main body of which would have suffered extensive casualties while trying to break through the first two lines. If the enemy managed to reach the third line in strength, then this line would act as a regrouping area and for reorganizing the reserves with the aim of launching a counterattack or to form a new defense line, depending on the tactical situation. The Soviets did not fully man the third line along its length. In areas of low threat there were insufficient troops before 4 July. The plans anticipated that, in the event that the first two lines were penetrated, the units manning them would withdraw to regroup in the army rear defense line, into which units from the reserves would already have deployed. In high threat areas, however, the third line was fully manned. The interrelationship between the three army defense lines can best be shown by the following example. The 13th Army was positioned on the north face of the salient, defending a 32km front with two corps in the first and another two in the second echelon. The 15th and 29th Corps manned the first two defense lines with a total of six rifle divisions. The 17th and 18th Guards Rifle Corps were deployed in the third

defense line, with the 17th Guards Rifle Corps covering the west end of the line. These corps bore the brunt of the XLVII Panzer Corps assault, which was unable to penetrate to the third defense line. The 17th Guards Rifle Corps moved forward to the second defense line, however, where a breach was reported, while the 280th and 132nd Rifle Divisions withdrew from the first line to the second, joining the 140th and 175th Rifle Divisions already there. The attack by the panzers was unable to overrun the area held by this massive force. In the center of the 13th Army sector, the 81st and 75th Rifle Divisions withdrew from the first to the second defense line and joined the 307th Rifle Division, which had been in Army reserve in the area of Ponyri. The eastern end of the Army sector was occupied by the 18th Guards Rifle Corps, consisting of the 2nd, 3rd, and 4th Guards Airborne Divisions. These élite formations took part in the battle as infantry since they lacked the basic means to conduct their operational missions, i.e., parachutes. When the Germans broke through the first defense line, the 8th and 148th Rifle Divisions withdrew to the second, joining the 74th Rifle Division. The 18th Guards Rifle Corps then moved forward to the second defense line, abandoning its positions in the third, to assist the defensive array and prevent a further enemy advance. The third defense line served as a base for strong counterattacks by the Central Front tank corps and 2nd Tank Army elements.

Behind the three first defense areas, manned by the forward armies, a further three main defense lines (called front defense lines) were constructed. These were designed to stop any possible German panzer penetrations and to serve as the base to launch counterattacks. In general, these lines were organized like the three first defense lines (army defense lines), with minefields and fortified positions. The fourth defense line (first front line) was located at a distance of between 50 and 100km from the frontline (primary defensive line) and was occupied, for most of its length, by Front troops. The fifth defense line (second front line) with the other two (first and third front lines) provided cut-off positions north and south of Kursk. This line was designed to provide the last defense of Kursk and a narrow corridor for the withdrawal of the defenders towards the city if the enemy reached that area. This line was unmanned before the battle. The sixth line followed the eastern bank of the Tim, Seym, and Oskol Rivers, along the base of the salient and it was also unmanned. While only one of these three lines was manned, it was by strong forces, deployed on the second front echelon and also with reserves. For example, the 2nd Tank Army, with two tank and one mechanized corps, was deployed in the second echelon of the Central Front. The Voronezh Front had the 1st Tank and the 69th Armies (the 69th with five rifle divisions) deployed in its second echelon. Each front was also reinforced with two independent tank corps and one mechanized corps in reserve. Soviet commanders were aware that if something did not go according to plan, they could also use the Steppe Front forces, especially the 5th Guards Tank Army. During the course of operation "Zitadelle," the Germans did manage to penetrate to the third defense line (out of the total of eight defense lines in the salient), but only at one point in the area of Prokhorovka. It was at Prokhorovka that the German advance was checked for good by the intervention of 5th Guards Tank Army

under the command of Pavel Alekseyevich Rotmistrov.

The German panzers were also successfully held back by the abundant use of mines. During the spring of 1943, the *Stavka* published a new directive on minefields and other obstacles. According to this directive, anti-tank minefields were to be sown to a depth of at least 100 meters. They were composed of three or more rows, 15 to 40 meters apart. Anti-tank mines were laid 6 to 10 meters apart, in order to avoid sympathetic detonation. In fact, the most extensive use of mines (anti-personnel and anti-tank) during World War II was during the Battle of Kursk (with El Alamein in second place). The most abundant use of anti-tank mines in the history of the war was reported to be in the defensive fortification of the salient. At least 280,000 anti-personnel and 290,000 anti-tank mines (the official Soviet history reports 637,000 mines at the start of the operations) were laid in the southern sector of the front, while, in the northern sector, more than 100,000 and 200,000 were laid respectively. The Soviets placed great emphasis on the mass use of mines, complying with the basic principle of the Zhukov plan, that of wearing down the attacker. The continual postponements of the attack gave the various commanders a great

The 76.2mm gun was the backbone of the Russian anti-tank defenses during the Kursk battle. Groups of five to 12 guns were formed into extremely efficient "Pakfronts" that put out of action hundreds of tanks and assault guns, slowing down the attacking forces' rate of advance.

A Soviet M-1942 (M-42) 45mm anti-tank gun that in reality was an upgrade of the M1930 37mm gun. This, in turn, was a version of the German Pak 35/36 (manufactured under German license) although the 45mm M1942 had a longer barrel. It also had spoked wheels instead of the usual solid steel wheel rims. It weighed 570kg, had a barrel length of 3m and it could penetrate 95mm armor at a range of 300m. It is uniformly finished in Dark Green. (Illustration by Dimitris Hadoulas/ Historical Notes by Stelios Demiras)

opportunity, around three months, to organize their defense more effectively by preparing extensive fields of death. Over 500,000 men assisted in the most extensive mine laying exercise ever on the Eastern Front. On the other hand, the Germans did not conduct any special training for clearing the Soviet minefields, as established estimates for breaking through minefield networks protecting fortified and very well protected areas was around four hours. At Kursk, German casualties from mines were serious, proving that the German Army had greatly underestimated the danger minefields could pose and that the Germans were grossly under-prepared for the successful clearing of the minefields.

Mines caused the loss of over 2,000 men (out of a total of 34,354). But where mines "excelled" was against the panzers. During the first two days of the battle, almost 200 tanks were put out of action, attesting to the attritional tactics conducted by the Soviets. Many of these damaged tanks were later repaired by the German maintenance units, only to fall victim once again. Minefields were laid with the view of slowing down the enemy, in combination with the construction of other obstacles and the general planning of the defense lines. Studies have shown that mines were more successful against armored targets than against personnel, managing to slow down armored forces but not the

infantry. The key to the successful use of minefields was the mass use of mines. Mine density in the southern sector was impressive, reaching 1,500 anti-tank and 1,700 anti-personnel mines per kilometer, covering the entire 164km length of the front. The frequency of the mines at Kursk was four times higher than at Stalingrad and six times higher than at Moscow. Minefields were mostly laid between the first and second defense lines and were integrated in the fortifications. Infantry, anti-tank guns and tanks were positioned between them. A third defense line behind them, also laid with minefields, was not really used because of events developing elsewhere. The greatest number of mines was laid along the first line (around 430,000 anti-tank and 410,000 anti-personnel), while the remainder (around 68,000 anti-tank and 28,000 anti-personnel) were distributed among the other defense lines. It should be noted that, on 30 June, with the imminent German attack looming, a further 10,000 mines were laid, while another 72,000 were added by 15 July. The death of the Commanding Officer of the 332nd Infantry Division (Lieutenant General Hans Schäfer), one of two high-ranking German officers killed during operation "Zitadelle," was from the effects of mine fragments.

Based on his experience, Field Marshal Zhukov gave priority to the

SOVIET ARTILLERY CONCENTRATION, 4 JULY 1943							
FRONT	ARMY	FRONTLINE LENGTH IN km	TOTAL NUMBER OF GUNS AND MORTARS	ARTILLERY CONCENTRATION PER km	ARTILLERY COMPOSITION		
					UNDER ARMY COMMAND	STAVKA RESERVES	ANTI-TANK GUNS
CENTRAL	48	38	991	26.0	241	80	321
	13	32	2,718	85.0	567	164	731
	70	62	1,585	25.5	361	122	483
	65	82	1,187	14.5	352	40	392
	60	92	905	9.8	171	48	219
Front Reserves	-	-	1,405	-	197	232	429
TOTAL	-	306	8,791	28.7	1,889	686	2,575
VORONEZH	38	80	904	11.3	139	100	239
	40	50	1,633	32.7	341	154	495
	6 Guards	64	1,674	26.2	331	258	589
	7 Guards	50	1,470	29.4	375	83	458
Front Reserves	-	-	2,538	-	359	220	575
TOTAL	-	244	8,219	33.6	1,545	815	2,360

defense-in-depth concept and so ordered the formation of the Steppe Front, which he placed under Ivan Stepanovich Konev. Konev's front deployed behind the salient and the *Stavka* strategic reserves were assigned to it. Five infantry armies (4th Guards Army under Lieutenant General Grigory Ivanovich Kulik, 5th Guards Army under Lieutenant General Aleksey Semyonovich Zhadov – assigned to the Voronezh Front on 8 July, the 27th Army under Lieutenant General Sergey Georgievich Trofimenko – assigned to the Voronezh Front on 14 July, the 53rd Army under Lieutenant General Ivan Mefodyevich Managarov – also

assigned to the Voronezh Front on 14 July, and the 47th Army of (then) Major General Pyotr Mikhaylovich Kozlov); one tank army (5th Guards Tank Army under Lieutenant General P. A. Rotmistrov – assigned to the Voronezh Front on 11 July, its 2nd Guards Tank Corps of Lieutenant General Aleksey Fyodorovich Popov – assigned to the Southwestern Front on 8 July); three independent tank corps (4th Guards Tank Corps under Major General Pavel Pavlovich Poluboyarov, 1st Mechanized Corps under Lieutenant General Mikhail Dmitrievich Solomatin, and the 3rd Guards Mechanized Corps under Major General Viktor Timofeevich

Soviet 76.2mm M1942 (ZiS-3) gun. This proved especially potent against enemy tanks, mainly when using high explosive (HE) rounds, though it was not designed as an anti-tank gun. Using HE or armor piercing (AP) rounds, it was capable of putting out of action any contemporary tank. It had a length of 4.179m and could penetrate 98mm armor at a range of 500m. The German forces captured a large number of these weapons during the 1941 invasion, with most of them being immediately put to use in various roles. This gun is uniformly finished in Dark Green. (Illustration by Dimitris Hadoulas/ Historical Notes by Stelios Demiras)

Obukhov); and three independent cavalry corps (3rd Guards Cavalry Corps under Lieutenant General Nikolay Sergeevich Oslikovsky, 5th Guards Cavalry Corps under Major General Aleksey Gordeevich Selivanov, and the 7th Guards Cavalry Corps under Major General Mikhail Fyodorovich Maleev). These forces were supported by the 5th Air Army commanded by Air Force General Sergey Kontratyevich Goryunov. This was the most powerful reserve force ever created by the USSR during World War II.

The salient's defense was assigned to the two highest commands, at army group level, covering, respectively, the northern and southern parts: a) the Central Front under General Konstantin Konstantinovich Rokossovsky with the 48th Army (Lieutenant General Prokofy Loginovich Romanenko), 13th Army (Lieutenant General Nikolay Pavlovich Pukhov), 70th Army (Lieutenant General Ivan Vasilyevich Galanin), 65th Army (Lieutenant General Pavel Ivanovich Batov), 60th Army (Lieutenant General Ivan Danilovich Chernyakhovsky), and the 2nd Tank Army (Lieutenant General Aleksey Grigoryevich Rodin). Rokossovsky's reserves consisted of two tank corps (9th Tank Corps under Lieutenant General Semyon Ilyich Bogdanov and the 19th Tank Corps of Lieutenant General Ivan Dmitrievich Vasilyev). The ground forces were supported by the 16th Air Army commanded by Lieutenant General (later, Marshal of Aviation) Sergey Ignatyevich Rudenko, and b) the Voronezh Front under the command of General Nikolay Vatutin with the 38th Army (Lieutenant General Nikandr Yevlampievich Chibisov), 40th Army (Lieutenant General Kirill Semyonovich

Moskalenko), 69th Army (Lieutenant General Vasily Dmitrievich Kryuchenkin), 1st Tank Army (Lieutenant General Mikhail Yefimovich Katukov), 6th Guards Army (ex-21st Army, Lieutenant General Ivan Mikhaylovich Chistyakov), and the 7th Guards Army (Lieutenant General Mikhail Stepanovich Shumilov). Vatutin's reserves consisted of a rifle corps (35th Guards Rifle Corps under Lieutenant General Sergey Georgievich Goryachev), and two tank corps (5th Guards Tank Corps under Lieutenant General Andrey Grigoryevich Kravchenko and the 2nd Guards Tank Corps under Lieutenant General Aleksey Semyonovich Burdeyny). The 2nd Air Army commanded by Marshal of Aviation Stepan Akimovich Krasovsky, was assigned to support these forces.

About 105,000 civilians contributed to this gigantic effort to construct the defensive network around Kursk, their numbers swelling to 300,000 by June. Over 5,000km of main and communication trenches were constructed in the Central Front area alone. In the town of Kursk, road blocks were built, 900 machine-gun nests constructed and selected buildings fortified. The same was done in the towns of Oboyan', Stary Oskol and other smaller towns. The Soviets had taken heed of the lessons taught them by the German masters of military art and their slaughter of thousands of troops and civilians. "Zitadelle" entered history as the fifth great German attack that once again practiced the doctrine of "lighting war" (*Blitzkrieg*), following Poland in 1939, France in 1940, Russia in 1941, and, again, in Russia in 1942. Kursk was the final curtain of the *Blitzkrieg* era.

Veterans' Evidence about the Soviet Fortifications

There was evidently a universal impression that all the German formations that took part in the attack had undergone many months of strenuous preparation in all kinds of operations. The reality, however, was something else. Training might have been tough, but there is no evidence that all the 16 divisions that took part in Operation "Zitadelle" underwent that tough training. Many of the infantry divisions were in the rear and were not given any training at all, while two of the panzer divisions only arrived in the area a short while before the operations began. Although there were veterans in the other seven panzer divisions, they have claimed that they were totally unaware of the type and/or extent of the Soviet defensive zone. Private Karl Stark served with the *Grossdeutschland* Panzer Grenadier Division engineer battalion and recounted in a 1999 interview, "There was some really tough training from March through June in our unit. This included general combat training together with training in assault squads. However, there were no combat exercises in conjunction with armor or armored infantry, also no live fire exercises. There was no training aimed specifically at the tasks anticipated during Operation "Zitadelle." We only learned later on that such an operation was imminent. We had no idea that the enemy's defensive systems had been built with such intensity until we came upon them during the actual attack. The main purpose of the training was to create strong unit cohesion." First Lieutenant Hans Joachim Jung was a 332nd Infantry Division anti-tank company commander: "I did see aerial photographs of the Soviet fortifications in the days before the offensive. I think our artillery had those. It clearly showed the anti-tank ditch, but the infantry positions were difficult to discern. Beside them were surely many 'fake' positions, although they could not be identified as such on the photographs. Minefields were not recognizable. The whole sector up to Cherkasskoye had been heavily fortified." In the *Grossdeutschland* sector they seemed to know what they were going to have to face, at least at battalion commander level. Captain Alfred Bergmann, commander of the 3rd Battalion/Infantry Regiment *Grossdeutschland* (a replacement commander from the third day of the operations, due to casualties sustained in the unit) recounts: "Our situation map in the operational department displayed a comprehensive view of the enemy situation at the end of June, beginning of July 1943. Several Soviet fortification systems positioned at substantial intervals towards the enemy's rear had been positively identified up to a depth of over 20km. We had a clear picture of the size of enemy artillery and anti-tank forces as well as numerous extended minefields. I realized at the time that it was pure nonsense to have our Panzer divisions target the most heavily fortified enemy positions head on and at such minimal clearance between each division. I was of the impression that many other officers of the divisional command were also aware of this." Joachim Buchardi, serving with the Artillery Regiment *Grossdeutschland* staff, comments: "My comrades and I had no idea at the time that we were set to attack a system of fortifications staggered in the enemy's depth and branched out over a wide area, which the enemy had been preparing for weeks on end and which featured deep ditches, earth bunkers, fixed flame throwers, dug-in tanks and countless mine obstacles, as we later discovered during the attack. We did not receive this intelligence about the enemy at that time."

The veterans' recollections clearly indicate that although the Germans were trained and had a general knowledge of what they would have to encounter, they were unaware of the specific details. They had no comprehensive battle maps and the idea they followed was that if they met with difficulties after the beginning of the operation, these would be solved by improvisations in accordance with the operational plan.

The Greatest Tank Battle in History - Kursk 1943

'Escape from Hell, Kursk 1943'. The panzer officer is armed with an MP 40 submachine gun and a Walther Pistol P38, which like the P08, was distributed to all ranks of the German Army. He wears the standard-issue black panzer uniform with old-style officers peaked cap *(Schirmmütze)* in field gray. He sports a Tank Assault badge. He and two surviving members of his Panther tank crew are trying to escape to their lines. Note the spare MP 40 magazines in his belt. The two privates are armed with a Walther Pistol P38 each, and wear a black double-breasted *Feldjacke* jacket with Trousers and *Feldmütze* cap. The private in the foreground sports a Tank Assault badge. (Painting by Johnny Shumate)

During the first two years of the war on the Eastern Front, the summers belonged to the *Wehrmacht* and the winters to the Red Army. When, finally, in the summer of 1943, the two protagonists had built up the cream of their forces for the decisive confrontation, very few people believed that the Soviets could withstand the most powerful concentration of Panzers ever assembled in history. The Panzers, however, failed to win and they would never again have the chance to gain new triumphs for the Third Reich. It is fair to say that the Soviets regarded Kursk as the Nazis' "Waterloo."

After 21 months of a merciless war between Germany and the Soviet Union, a strange, almost unnatural calm reigned on the Eastern Front in April 1943. Both sides had reasons to yearn for a respite from the deadly battle that the Germans had launched with their invasion on 22 June 1941. Much had changed since that first summer of the German-Soviet war, however, when the panzers had almost annihilated the massive but inexperienced forces of the Red Army and nearly reached the gates of Moscow. Checked for the first time ever in front of the Russian capital, the Germans regrouped and then, in the summer of 1942, launched an attack in the southern part of the front, threatening to capture the Caucasus oilfields on which the Soviet economy depended. At the same time, the *Wehrmacht* attempted to cut the great river artery of the Volga and, thus, deprive the USSR of one of its main axes of communications.

The Germans could not undertake such a venture alone and committed the fatal error of enrolling their "satellite" troops (Hungarians, Italians, Romanians, etc.) to cover the flanks of their deep advance. This fundamental mistake, one of many to result from Hitler's impulsive interference in the conduct of operations, forced the German 6th Army to stall in the rubble of Stalingrad (while its flanks were covered by its inadequate allies). There, on 19 November 1942, a massive Soviet counterattack annihilated the German force, producing catastrophic casualties. The weeks between the encirclement and the crushing defeat of Friedrich von Paulus' army were among the most hectic for the *Wehrmacht* High Command (OKW) and the Army High Command (OKH), as they charted the fast-moving Soviet columns that were encircling whole army groups. The Russian armies then turned to liberate Rostov, the Caucasus, Kursk, Belgorod, and Khar'kov, and to continue to beat a triumphal drive towards the Dnieper passes. It was clear that Stalin and the General Headquarters of the Soviet Armed Forces (*Stavka*) did not just plan to wipe out the already condemned 6th Army (its agony finally ended on 2 February 1943) but to extend their

Adolf Hitler looks at a map while listening carefully to the set daily briefing about the operations on the Eastern Front. General Kurt Zeitzler, the Chief of Staff since September 1942 and the man behind Operation "Zitadelle" (Citadel), is on the left.

Comparing the two dictators, Stalin definitely had more extensive experience of war than Hitler and he also sought, and took, advice from his generals.

counterattack in the hope of annihilating all German forces on the southern front and regaining all of the Ukraine.

Manstein saves the *Wehrmacht*

The Soviets' triumphal march was finally checked thanks to Field Marshal Erich von Manstein, an officer in the classic Prussian tradition, who had the gift of remaining calm and retaining a clear mind even in the most adverse conditions. Manstein performed another of the "tricks" that had made him world-famous as a dangerous, unpredictable opponent. He patiently and methodically regrouped the remaining German forces that had withdrawn from the Caucasus, and reinforced them with newly formed divisions that had been rushed in from France. He then attacked the Soviets when their lines were over-extended, smashed their vanguards, forced their mechanized forces to retreat, and recaptured Khar'kov, the Soviets' fourth largest city, which the *Wehrmacht* had lost just a few weeks earlier, on 15 March 1943. This amazing counterattack ground to a halt after the capture of Belgorod, a major town in southwestern Russia, because of the onset of the season of rain and mud – the dreadful spring *"rasputitsa,"* when rain and melting snow turn the earth into mud and the entire Russian steppe becomes a quagmire. The two protagonists had to satisfy themselves with the ground they had gained and wait for the land to dry while planning for the future.

Although the Soviet counterattack after Stalingrad had ultimately come to a halt, nothing could overshadow its success in managing to eliminate an entire German Army in the city on the Volga and, for the first time in history, capture a German field marshal. It is true that the Soviets had already learnt much from their previous defeats, but Manstein's unexpected counterattack at Khar'kov was a salutary lesson for Stalin himself, who like almost all dictators, had a taste for imposing specific strategies and operational tactics on his generals. After this setback, he became less arrogant and was eager, for the first time, to let his army commanders work without him, limiting himself to overseeing *Stavka* planning and to capitalizing fully on the experience of his outstanding staff officers.

Stavka came to some useful conclusions concerning the reasons for its failure and defeat at Khar'kov. The Soviet general staff carefully, coldly, and logically analyzed the reasons for the loss, at the same time giving the *Wehrmacht* a chance to stabilize its fluid front and boost its morale. One of the reasons was that the Germans were able to use a more concentrated railroad network in the occupied Russian territories than that used by the Soviets farther to the east. The communication network shrank the further one moved towards the Urals. At least five railroad lines on the North-South axis and nine on the East-West were being used by the German Army between Moscow and the Sea of Azov, while the Red Army had, through sheer desperation, just managed to establish itself in Kursk by using a single railroad line. This line connected Moscow and Stalingrad via Yelets, with a branch leading from Voronezh to Kursk through Kastornoye. Another usable line lay east of the Don River:

At Hitler's insistence, General Heinz Guderian took on the job of Inspector-General of Panzer Troops in February 1943. In that capacity, Guderian pressed for an increase in the monthly production of new tank types and personally oversaw the panzer divisions' reorganization. Here he inspects a Tiger tank of the 2nd SS Panzer Grenadier Division *Das Reich*.

Voronezh - Liski - Rossosh' - but it took more time to move forces and matériel that way. So, while the Red Army could move 1.5 divisions per day, the Germans were able to move at least 3.5 in the North/South axis and more than six on the West/East axis.

The inadequacy of the railroad network almost precipitated a crushing defeat for the Red Army when Manstein launched his counterattack. The *Stavka* ordered General Konstantin Rokossovsky to move the entire Don Front, of which he was commander-in-chief and which had just completed the mopping up operations in Stalingrad, from there on the banks of the Volga, to the area north of Kursk. Rokossovsky was to reposition the Don Front between the Bryansk and the Voronezh Fronts to reinforce the area north of Khar'kov. Redeploying the forces in time using a single railroad line was unfeasible. It was calculated that, with an average 65 carriages per train, a mechanized brigade would require seven trains, a tank corps 20, a cavalry division 18, and a rifle division 15. So, it was no surprise that it was impossible for the Central Front (the renamed Don Front) to help the other Soviet forces that were attempting to check Manstein.

German transport superiority by itself would not have mattered at all if, on the other hand, the *Wehrmacht* had not had sufficient reserves in the spring of 1943 to undertake a major counterattack. Manstein was lucky to have two large troop reserves able to bolster the forces needed for such an operation. Having lost 20 of its most battle-hardened divisions at Stalingrad and another six in the battles of the River Don, the OKH decided to evacuate the Rzhev salient, shortening the length of its frontage in that area by 368km, in order to be able to utilize the entire 22 divisions of the 9th Army and position it north of Kursk, close to Oryol. The Demyansk salient was evacuated in the same way.

An even larger reserve of German forces was to be found in France – where formations that had suffered major casualties on the Eastern Front were sent to recuperate and rearm. Ten of these divisions were hurried back to Russia during the winter of

German Tiger I Ausf E heavy tank, 8th Company (8/sPzKp,) 3rd SS Panzer Grenadier Division *Totenkopf*, Kursk, 1943. The Tiger was heavy in both firepower and armor, but was not designed with the advantages of the T-34's sloped armor. It could overcome any Soviet tank and so was positioned as the spearhead of the attacks at Kursk along with the Panthers and Ferdinands. When the mass Soviet defenses limited its mobility it fell prey to Russian anti-tank defenses due to its thin side and rear armor. Another of its major disadvantages became apparent during its transportation to the front, by road or rail, and that was its large width. Its battle weight was 57 tons, its maximum speed 45.5km/h, and it carried a five-member crew. It was armed with an 88mm gun and two 7.92mm machine guns and had a maximum armor thickness of 110mm. This tank is finished in a two-color scheme with Sand Yellow as

1942-43 to assist in re-establishing the front, while a further seven were sent back between April and June 1943 to take part in the next large offensive. This mass movement of German reinforcements from France did not go unnoticed by the Soviets, who complained bitterly to their Western Allies about the Anglo-Americans' continued failure to open the long-awaited "Second Front" on continental Europe.

Stalin was justified in his protestations. Hitler would not have been able to move so many reinforcements to the Eastern Front, practically denuding his Western European defenses, if he were not absolutely sure that no invasion threatened France during 1943. In fact, there was just one fully combat-ready *Wehrmacht* division in France during the summer of 1943, the 65th Infantry Division, with the remainder of the units being the remnants of formations that had been disbanded in Russia.

Faced with the need to defend the huge empire he had created, Hitler focused on securing numerical superiority in manpower, setting aside the actual fighting quality of his formations. He decided to reconstitute the 20 divisions that had been lost at

Stalingrad, and to form a further 16 that would be used to cover the departure of the experienced divisions from France. This "inflationary" measure resulted in the main portion of the recruits being assigned to these new formations, while the already existing fighting divisions on the Eastern Front received practically no manpower reinforcements. In consequence, many of the divisions on the Eastern front were under strength, comprising fewer than the nine infantry battalions required by the German organization table.

The *Wehrmacht's* strategic problem in the spring of 1943

By shortening its front in the north, the *Wehrmacht* had gained a defensive advantage. But this advantage vanished after Manstein's successful counterattack in the south whetted Hitler's appetite for further conquests. The successful Khar'kov campaign destroyed any of the German generals' lingering hopes that Hitler might sanction a tactical retreat to the west where, behind a naturally fortified defense line, the *Wehrmacht* might

the basic color and irregular stripes in Red Brown. (Illustration by Dimitris Hadoulas/ Historical Notes by Stelios Demiras)

**SOVIET TANK OFFICER, 2nd TANK ARMY,
CENTRAL FRONT, KURSK 1943.**
He wears the 1943 pattern *gimnastyorka* (shirt-tunic) in khaki
color with stand up collar with gilt buttons and shoulder
boards, *sharovary* (trousers) in same color with "semi-
breeches" in diamond shape with reinforcing patch at the
knee. On his feet are black leather boots. At the start of WWII
the tankers' headgear was from brown leather but in the end
was made from black canvas. Note the red piping on shoulder
boards for tank crewmen. Usually officers were armed with a
7.62mm Tokarev pistol TT33 not shown here. (Illustration
by Johnny Shumate / Historical Notes-Comments
by Stelios Demiras)

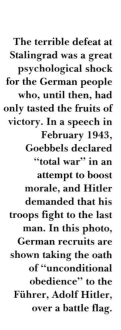

The terrible defeat at Stalingrad was a great psychological shock for the German people who, until then, had only tasted the fruits of victory. In a speech in February 1943, Goebbels declared "total war" in an attempt to boost morale, and Hitler demanded that his troops fight to the last man. In this photo, German recruits are shown taking the oath of "unconditional obedience" to the Führer, Adolf Hitler, over a battle flag.

reorganize away from Soviet harassment. The tidal wave of Manstein's counterattack provided, according to Liddell Hart, "a new-old set of offensive springboards that looked all too promising to a man whose instincts were predominantly offensive, and whose mind was intensely reluctant to give up the idea that an offensive gamble might still turn the whole situation in his favor."

The re-invigorated *Wehrmacht* had, to an extent, exacted revenge for Stalingrad. New units – including the three *Waffen SS* divisions – Hitler's bodyguard, the *Leibstandarte Adolf Hitler*; *Das Reich*; and the *Totenkopf* 'Death's Head' – arrived from France in February to form Manstein's "Iron Fist." The German forces were occupying nearly the same positions they had held prior to their spring

offensive the year before – the beginning of the Stalingrad venture. They felt they had no reason to abandon the industrialized, mineral-rich Donets Basin.

On 11 April 1943, the Chief of the General Staff, General Kurt Zeitzler, handed a plan to Adolf Hitler. The general had conceived a re-launch of the Russian adventure with an attack, although the ideas it contained were neither inspired nor original. A quick look at the map revealed that the existing frontline had a huge bulge on the German side in the area of Kursk, an extensive, almost rectangular salient, with a front of 170km and a depth of about 110km. This salient was ripe for elimination along with all the Soviet forces in it. The OKH was mesmerized by this opportunity for a time-honored flanking attack. Having retained Oryol to the north of the salient, and having recaptured Belgorod to its south, the *Wehrmacht* was in position to launch a classic pincer attack against Soviet positions around Kursk. By cutting off the Red Army forces inside the great salient (where, intelligence reported, the Soviets had at least ten armies), a breach of huge dimensions would be opened on the Eastern Front and the panzer divisions would, once again, be able to drive eastwards, recreating the fluid situation that bodes well for offensive operations. In addition, thousands of Soviet troops would be captured and sent as slave labor to Germany where they would serve the Reich's war industry.

Having no alternative plan, Hitler agreed to the attack and issued Operational Order No. 6 on 15 April, further requesting that the *Wehrmacht* "proceed to preparations with the utmost attention and energy. The best formations, the best armies, the finest commanders, and huge quantities of ammunition have to be positioned in appropriate places. Every officer and soldier should be absolutely convinced of the importance of this attack. The victory in Kursk must light a beacon for the whole world." The initial launch date for the attack was 3 May 1943. At the end of April, however, Hitler changed his mind and postponed the date, first until 5 May, and then to 9 May 1943.

By the winter of 1942-43, the Red Army was not only larger, but it was also more powerful than the OKH believed. Hitler was convinced, on the contrary, that by this time the enemy should have reached the limits of their endurance and be ready to collapse due to the crushing casualties they had suffered. One final blow by the *Wehrmacht* would result in such a decisive defeat that the Red Army

Soviet officers study the battle plan on a model. They are wearing new type uniforms and their rank insignia are on the shoulder boards (*pogon*), a system used in the Tsarist period that was re-introduced in the Red Army during 1943.

would be annihilated, Hitler believed. The Eastern Front would then be stabilized for a year or more; Stalin would, in all probability, sue for a separate peace, and the Reich would be free to turn its attention to the west, to face the Anglo-Americans with no distractions, because it was clear that they were preparing for a landing against the Axis in an unknown area of the Mediterranean.

"How many people in the world know where Kursk is?"

The German generals, however, were divided over the proposed plan. A large number of the more experienced commanders had already begun to have serious doubts; they even questioned the possibility of defeating the USSR. For Hitler, meanwhile, the views of the generals directly involved with the "Zitadelle" (Citadel) operation

A Soviet KV-1S heavy tank in the area of Kursk-Oryol during 1943. The KV-1S was a Soviet attempt to reduce the weight of the KV-1 series of tanks by about five tons. The most important changes were the mounting of a much smaller turret and the reduction of its deck armor to 75mm (the KV-1 Model 42 had 90mm). Lighter wheels were also used in at least two variants. It was armed with the 76.2mm F34 (ZiS-5) gun and three 7.62mm DT machine guns. Production of the KV-1S ended in April 1943 after 1,370 units had been built. It proved incapable of facing the Tiger and Panther in the Kursk-Oryol battle. This is a KV-1S uniformly finished in Dark Green. The name "I. D. Papanin" is inscribed next to the tank code. (Illustration by Dimitris Hadoulas/Historical Note by Stelios Demiras)

were the most important. Field Marshal Günther von Kluge (Commander-in-Chief, Army Group Center) had assigned the 9th Army (General Officer Commanding, General Walter Model) to the northern pincer of the operation. Field Marshal Manstein, having recently won acclaim, was in charge of Army Group South and he was assigned the reorganized and powerful 4th Panzer Army (General Hermann Hoth) and Army Group Kempf under General Werner Kempf.

Great emphasis was placed on the views of General Heinz Guderian, the "armored magician," who had practically "dragged" the German Army in 1940 to one of the most amazing victories of all time: the elimination of the British and French armies with a real "sickle cut" from Sedan to Abbeville. This faithful soldier had one major disadvantage: he freely and fearlessly expressed his opinions while Hitler could brook no dissent. When Guderian's 2nd Panzer Army was checked a few dozen kilometers from Moscow around Christmas in1941, Hitler sacked the general. After Germany's resounding failure at Stalingrad exposed the sorry state of the Panzer forces, Hitler asked yet again for the services of Guderian, who

by then was suffering heart problems. On 28 February 1943, Guderian was appointed Inspector-General of Panzer Troops – a post that the general accepted only on condition that he report directly and exclusively to Hitler.

The first issue that Guderian had to tackle was the feasibility of another *Wehrmacht* attack on the Eastern Front in 1943. After receiving briefings on the readiness, manpower, and equipment of the Panzer divisions, Guderian declared that he was totally against the operation. He preferred that the *Wehrmacht* content itself with stabilized defense throughout 1943, thus allowing itself time to reorganize its Panzer forces to be ready to take up the initiative for action in 1944. Losses from previous operations had decimated the Panzer divisions, which possessed but few tanks, and those qualitatively inferior to the Soviet models. Experienced officers were in short supply as well, with only a small number available. On the other hand, German factories had started producing new tank types: the heavy 57-ton Tigers armed with the 8.8cm gun, and the medium 43-ton Panther with the high-velocity 75mm gun. In addition, the eccentric Professor

Ferdinand Porsche, whom Hitler greatly respected, had built a new, heavy, 65-ton, self-propelled gun that was named after him, although he had lost the competition for the Tiger tank. These new armored vehicles exuded sufficient promise for the future for the *Wehrmacht* to have a qualitative superiority in tanks for the first time on the Eastern Front. Problems still remained in the production of these new highly complex and costly weapons, and the production lines could only complete 25 Tigers and 50 Panthers per month, excellent design and firepower notwithstanding. More important, these new tanks, in particular the Panther, suffered from what Guderian called "teething troubles."

At first, Hitler was wary of Operation "Zitadelle." He called a conference of the highest military leadership in Munich on 4 May, following a briefing on General Model's report, in which he expressed his objections (his main argument being *Luftwaffe* reconnaissance-photos that revealed the enormous extent of the Soviet defensive fortifications in the salient). Field Marshal Wilhelm Keitel and General Alfred Jodl from OKW, Zeitzler as the OKH representative,

Kluge, Manstein, Guderian, Model, the *Luftwaffe* Chief-of-Staff, General of the Air Force Hans Jeschonnek, and the Armament Minister, Albert Speer, took part in this conference. Following a 45-minute monologue, Hitler announced that he had decided to postpone the attack for at least six weeks in order to give the Panzer divisions time to be equipped with more Tigers and Panthers that everyone believed would easily be able to knock out the Soviet T-34s. Although at the time, Soviet factories were rolling out at least 2,000 new tanks for the Red Army each month, no one objected to delaying the offensive. Guderian reiterated his belief that the new tanks should only be used in battle when they were available in large quantities. Model expressed the view that the Soviets already knew everything about the planned German offensive and were preparing to launch a pre-emptive attack of their own, for which the Germans could simply wait. Manstein, on the other hand, always especially sparing in his words when talking with Hitler, simply remarked that the chances for a successful operation would be less at the beginning of July than at the beginning of May.

Without doubt, this issue was of great concern to Hitler, but he was

German 15cm *Schwere Panzerhaubitze auf Geschützwagen III/IV (Sf)* or *Hummel (Bumble-Bee)*, self-propelled heavy howitzer on tracked carriage, 9th Panzer Division, Kursk, July 1943. It was armed with a 15cm sFH18/1 L/30 gun and one 7.92mm MG 34 machine gun. It had a combat weight of 24 tons, a speed of 42km/h, and carried a six-man crew. By May 1943, 100 Hummeln were to be built for use in the planned summer offensive. The Hummel was issued to the heavy batteries of the armored artillery detachments (SP) of several Panzer Divisions early in 1943 and first saw action in the Battle of Kursk. This *Hummel* is finished in a two-color camouflage scheme with Sand Yellow as the base color and irregularly shaped, over-painted patches of Dark Green. (Illustration by Dimitris Hadoulas/ Historical Notes by Stelios Demiras)

In the foreground, General Hermann Hoth is seen studying enemy positions through artillery binoculars. He was the General Officer Commanding 4th Panzer Army in the summer of 1943 and his Army was the most élite and potent strike force ever assembled by the Third Reich.

under intense pressure from his immediate subordinates, mostly from Zeitzler. A new conference was convened on 10 May 1943, and once again Guderian offered reasons why the *Wehrmacht* should not attack towards the east in 1943. The OKW Chief, Field Marshal Keitel, responded that "for political reasons" it was necessary to go ahead and launch the operation. These comments caused the professional Guderian to explode: "Is it really necessary to attack Kursk, and indeed in the east in 1943 at all? Do you think anyone even knows where Kursk is? The entire world doesn't care if we capture Kursk or not. What is the reason that is forcing us to launch an attack this year on Kursk, or even more, on the Eastern Front?" Hitler, following this heated exchange, simply replied: "I know. The thought of it turns my stomach."

The idea of passively waiting on the Eastern Front was an anathema to Hitler, however. He knew only too well that his dictatorial regime did not have the luxury of remaining idle, as that could well lead to his political elimination. He had to take the initiative, and for that reason he rejected Guderian's arguments, although he agreed they were very reasonable.

There were other arguments concerning the operation, if the *Wehrmacht* had to definitely attack. Manstein proposed in return, after having been briefed on Zeitzler's plan, his own version of the "elastic" defense, given that the Soviets were sure to

resume their attacks after the muddy season, Manstein wanted to take advantage of the enemy operations, allowing them to develop up to the River Dnieper, drawing the Soviets deep into the Ukraine, and then striking at their flanks and rear with the reserves he would position close to Kiev. This plan proposed a counterattack of a similar concept, but on a larger scale than the one he had conducted during the spring. Hitler, however, was not "the man who would risk much in strategy," according to Manstein, and the Führer rejected this solution, as he did not want to lose the Donets Basin, which was of great economic importance. Finally, he set the date of the attack for 3 July 1943, although at the end of June, he again postponed the operation until 5 July.

Both Kluge and Manstein remained hopeful of the chances of success, despite the continuous postponements of "Zitadelle." As Liddell Hart has commented: "Hope is commonly fostered by professional opportunity. Keen soldiers have a natural inclination to develop faith in a venture of which they are placed in charge and a natural reluctance to express doubts that would weaken a superior's faith in their powers." Zeitzler had high hopes for his plan. He believed that with two convergent blows from north and south, allied to the surprise and mass use of the heavy Tiger and Panther tanks and the massive Ferdinand tank hunters, the Panzers would be able to surround and eliminate the Central and Voronezh Front troops in the Kursk salient in a few days.

The Eastern Front may have temporarily remained idle, but the World War was marked by great developments elsewhere between April and June 1943. At the beginning of May, the renowned Panzer Army Afrika (without the presence of its

One of the primary reasons behind the postponement of the German attack until the beginning of July 1943 was Hitler's insistence on strengthening the assault units with more of the new Tiger and Panther tanks. This photo shows Tigers reaching the front on special railcars.

talented leader, Field Marshal Erwin Rommel) and its 275,000 battle-hardened Axis troops surrendered to the Western Allies in Tunisia. This made the Anglo-Americans eager for a jump onto continental Europe. In the meantime, the skies over the Third Reich had been turned into a merciless aerial battlefield with the airborne armadas of the Americans hammering Germany by day and the British by night. The RAF continued to bomb the vital Ruhr industrial area in May, after having destroyed the Ruhr Dams in a skillful raid. Also targeted were V-1 missile installations at Peenemünde. At sea, Admiral Karl Dönitz's submarine war appeared to have stalled. May was the month that saw a decisive defeat of the U-boats, with the unprecedented loss of 41 submarines, forcing the survivors to withdraw from the mid-Atlantic to the safer waters around the Azores to regroup. Even in the maelstrom of war, however, politics were still part of the game. On 13 April, the Germans announced the discovery of mass graves of 14,000 executed Polish officers, missing since 1939, in the Katyn' Forest, near Smolensk, in Russia. The Soviets

denounced the reports as Nazi propaganda and the Western Allies quickly suppressed the news in the name of the common cause against Germany.

"Total War"

On 18 February 1943, the German Minister for Propaganda, Joseph Goebbels, made an explosive speech in the Berlin Sportspalast, where he declared "Total War" with the "consent" of the German people by acclamation. Following Stalingrad, the Nazi leadership had been forced to reconsider its views on how long the war would last and to realize that it could not hope to emerge triumphant unless all the Reich's resources (economy, manpower, etc.) were dedicated to the fight.

The length of the work week throughout Germany was increased to 60 hours, deferment from army service for educational reasons was abolished, and all males between 16 and 65 years old, as well as women between 17 and 45, were to be available, at any time, for any kind of service within the framework of the military effort. Hitler

German *Schwere Panzerspahwagen (SdKfz 232) 8 Rad*, **heavy cross-country armoured car 88th** *Panzer Aufklarungs Abteilung*, **18th Panzer Division, Kursk 1943. It was armed with 2cm KwK30 (or 38) gun and one 7.92mm MG34 machine gun. It had a combat weight of 8.3 tons, a speed of 85km/h, and carried a four-man crew. It is finished in a two-color scheme with Sand Yellow as the basic color and irregular shaped over-painted patches in Olive Green. (Illustration by Dimitris Hadoulas/ Historical Notes by Stelios Demiras)**

Youth members would cultivate the fields and would help bring in the harvest; 1.5 million women would take on various occupations in order to free industrial workers for war production; while prisoners would be set to work for the war as well. Any businesses having no direct connection with the war effort (e.g. night clubs, restaurants, jewelers, fashion houses, etc.), were forced to close down and their employees transferred to more pressing needs. Simultaneously, the work hours were excessively increased for the 6.3 million unfortunate foreign workers, most of whom were forced labor working in the industries of the Third Reich.

Next came the moment for the *Wehrmacht's* reorganization. OKW estimated that 800,000 conscripts were needed to cover the heavy losses sustained during the winter of 1942-43 (an estimated 1,135,000 men were lost by the *Wehrmacht* on the Eastern Front between 1 June 1942 and 30 June 1943) and Hitler took great care to secure that number with his diktats. Young men born in 1925 (18-year old men) were called to arms a few months before their call up would previously have been due (a total of about 400,000 men). Another 200,000 men were

found in categories previously exempt from military service, including miners, those in non-military industries, heads of large families, and soldiers who had recovered from serious wounds. The conscription of age groups of 21-37 and 38-42 gathered in the remaining 200,000 men required. By drawing on this pool of manpower, on 30 May 1943, the *Wehrmacht* reached the apex of its numerical strength since the start of the war, fielding 3,403,000 men in combat units on the Eastern Front – 11 per cent more troops than during the beginning of Operation "Barbarossa." These forces were fully equipped, thanks to Speer's more than two-fold increase in weapons production. During 1943, the Germans built 9,200 tanks and assault guns (against 4,300 in 1942), while production of heavy guns increased from 1,200 to 2,600. The Reich proved that it was far from being beaten.

The Soviets Reorganize

The Soviets were not idle either. They made the most of the pause in operations during the spring of 1943, and quickly began reorganizing the army. The Red Army's high command

PANZER OFFICER - *MAJOR* **STANDING
IN THE COPULA OF A TIGER I TANK, PANZER
GRENADIER DIVISION** *GROSSDEUTSCHLAND,*
KURSK 1943

He wears the officer's pattern black *Feldmütze* with
silver cord twist piping, *Feldjacke* double breasted
jacket with Gilt 'GD' cipher pinned to the shoulder
straps. He sports a Knights Cross (around neck) to
his Iron Cross, an Iron Cross 1st Class (on jacket)
and the ribbons of Iron Cross 2nd Class over his
"Winter Campaign" Medal 1941-1942 (through his
lapel button hole), a Tank Assault badge, and
Eastern and Western front ribbons. On his right
sleeve is seen the cuff title *Grossdeutschland*. He is
armed with Walther Pistol P38 with holster. Note
the throat microphone with the headset and
Hensoldt field glasses. (Illustration by Johnny
Shumate / Historical Notes-Comments
by Stelios Demiras)

was, by then, more experienced and those generals who had not proven up to the job had been removed by the process of natural selection so rigorously practiced by Stalin. The drastic removal of the leaders of 1941 had created space for a new generation of energetic generals in the higher ranks, most of them under 40 years of age. In addition, each revealed a much higher level of professionalism compared to his predecessors. Moreover, at least 250,000 junior officers who had been wounded early in the war had returned to the ranks by mid-1943, passing on their experience to the units, while a number of well-trained cadres graduated from the military schools. The union of a younger, more highly-trained leadership in combination with the battle experience of the troops soon showed at all levels, from staff work to skilful tactics on the battlefield.

Conscripts were called up twice a year, in spring and autumn, producing 3 million men, aged 17. At the same time, 40 percent of the USSR's population remained under German occupation. The Soviets were pioneers in the use of large numbers of women in the Armed Forces, including in combat positions. This measure was taken to compensate for the tremendous losses the country had sustained during previous battles. In consequence, shortly before the Battle of Kursk, the total number of the Red Army personnel in combat units reached 6,724,000 men and women. Nevertheless, the Soviets were still forced to reduce the strength of the classic infantry division to 9,380 personnel, while retaining all the heavy infantry weapons and arming one in five men with an automatic weapon (the ratio in 1941 was 1:37).

The number of divisions increased from 407 on 31 December 1942, to 462 in July 1943. Twenty-five artillery divisions, 27 independent anti-tank brigades (each equipped with 50-70 guns and one infantry battalion), and 163 independent anti-tank regiments (each with 20-24 guns of 76mm and 45mm) were formed. After having been on the bitter receiving end of *Luftwaffe* strikes during previous battles, the formations were reinforced with 183 independent anti-aircraft artillery regiments and 36 anti-aircraft divisions whose mission was to create a "wall of steel" above the friendly fighting troops. As for armor, the five tank armies were strengthened with more tanks and mechanized infantry and each fielded around 600 tanks. This, however, was still not enough for *Stavka*, and 24 independent tank corps were formed, each with 10,977 men, 253 tanks and *Samokhodnaya Ustanovka* (SU) self-propelled guns, 60 towed guns and mortars, and eight multiple rocket launchers. Furthermore, each of these formations was accompanied by 13 mechanized corps (each of 15,018 men, 229 tanks and self-propelled guns, 108 guns and mortars, and eight multiple rocket launchers). The Soviets firmly believed in the flexibility offered by many small, independent armored units and they still had 101 independent tank brigades and 110 independent tank regiments on 1 July 1943. Moreover, they formed 13 new independent assault gun regiments equipped with the SU series. These armored vehicles had no turret but the three different variants were armed with 76mm, 122mm, and 152mm guns that were a deadly threat even to the heavier German tanks.

This potential of the Red Army to raise the number of its units was due to the fact that the Soviet economy was racing ahead at an unbelievable pace. Russian oil production, which had fallen from 33 million tons in 1941 to

Battle fatigue and anxiety are clearly shown in the faces of the SS *Totenkopf* Division troops. Despite their best efforts, they were unable to break through the Soviet defenses north of the Psyol River.

18 million tons at the beginning of 1943, showed signs of recovery. The railroad network was quickly being repaired in the liberated areas and weapon production in the factories beyond the Ural Mountains rocketed: in 1943, the country manufactured 3,400,000 rifles, 2,060,000 submachine guns, 250,000 light machine-guns, 90,500 heavy machine-guns, 12,200 anti-aircraft guns, 22,100 large-caliber guns and 22,900 tanks and assault guns, which were the equal, if not better, than anything produced by the *Wehrmacht* until then (the exception being the new German heavy tanks). While the Red Army might have had excellent weapons in abundant quantities, it still lacked complementary material (such as radios), and mostly motor transport, a weakness met by an increasing stream of Lend-Lease American trucks. Liddell Hart comments: "Hardly less important for mobility was the quantity of American canned food that was poured in, for it also helped to solve the supply problem that, because of the huge size of Russia's forces and the scarcity of communications, formed the biggest check on her capacity to exert her strength."

An Iron Ring Around Kursk

By 5 July 1943, the Germans had managed to assemble around the Kursk salient the most impressive armored mass the world had ever witnessed. Out of the 50 divisions that would take part in Operation "Zitadelle," nine had been withdrawn from the Rzhev salient, 13 had been transferred to the Eastern Front from France over the previous six months, and 10 panzer or panzer grenadier divisions were also amassed, leaving Army Groups Center and North with practically no reserves, thus making them extremely vulnerable to Soviet counterattacks in the immediate future.

German *Panzerkampfwagen III Ausf M (SdKfz 141/1)* medium tank, 29th Panzer Regiment, 12th Panzer Division, Kursk, July 1943. Although not so effective in frontal tank-versus-tank actions, there were still 432 PzKpfw III (with 5cm KwK L/60) with Army Groups Center and South at the start of the offensive at Kursk in July 1943. It was armed with a 5cm KwK39 L/60 gun and two 7.92mm MG 34 machine guns. This tank is finished in a three-color camouflage scheme with Sand Yellow as the base color and irregularly shaped over-painted patches of Red Brown and Dark Green. The three-digit tank code was painted on sides and rear of the turret. (Illustration by Dimitris Hadoulas/Historical Notes by Stelios Demiras)

Of the remaining 18 divisions, seven were extremely weak and would take care of passive defense under the 2nd Army.

The order of battle on the northern face of the salient from east to west was: 229th Infantry Division (under Lieutenant General Ralph Graf von Oriola, with six infantry battalions), the only 2nd Panzer Army division that would take part in the operation. Then Model's 9th Army formations followed. XXIII Corps (General Johannes Friessner) with the 78th Assault Division (Lieutenant General Hans Traut, with six battalions and 50 armored vehicles), the 216th Infantry Division (Major General Friedrich-August Schack, six battalions), and the 383rd Infantry Division (Major General Edmund Hoffmeister, at full-strength with nine battalions). XLI Panzer Corps (General Josef Harpe) arrayed the 86th Infantry Division (Lieutenant General Helmuth Weidling, with six battalions), the 292nd Infantry Division (Lieutenant General Wolfgang von Kluge, with six battalions), and the 18th Panzer Division (Major General Karl-Wilhelm von Schlieben, with only 75 tanks). Model decided to reinforce the weakened XLI Panzer Corps with the 656th Tank Hunter Regiment of

Lieutenant Colonel Ernst Geduld Freiherr von Jugenfeld that was equipped with 90 Ferdinand self-propelled tank destroyers, the only ones of the type that would be used in the Battle of Kursk.

XLVII Panzer Corps (General Joachim Lemelsen) fielded, in the first line, the 6th Infantry Division (Lieutenant General Horst Grossmann, with nine battalions) and the 20th Panzer Division (Major General Mortimer von Kessel, with 85 tanks). Two other battle-hardened formations were kept as reserves halfway between the front line and Oryol: the 2nd Panzer Division (Lieutenant General Vollrath Lübbe, with 136 tanks, including 40 Panthers), and the 9th Panzer Division (Lieutenant General Walter Scheller, with 111 tanks). Many artillery units were attached to the corps, as was the 505th Heavy Tank Battalion that was equipped with 20 Tigers and 25 PzKpfw III. The XLVII Panzer Corps was Model's main strike force.

The XLVI Panzer Corps (General Hans Zorn) was a panzer corps in name only, since it possessed no panzer divisions. It was composed of the 31st Infantry Division (Lieutenant General Friedrich Hossbach, with six infantry

Hadoulas

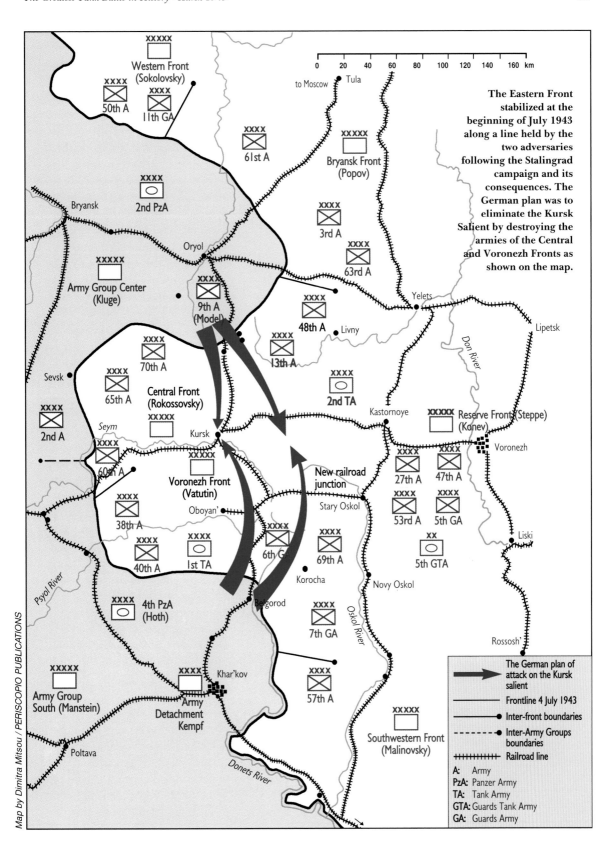

The Eastern Front stabilized at the beginning of July 1943 along a line held by the two adversaries following the Stalingrad campaign and its consequences. The German plan was to eliminate the Kursk Salient by destroying the armies of the Central and Voronezh Fronts as shown on the map.

Western Front (Sokolovsky)

50th A

11th GA

61st A

Bryansk Front (Popov)

2nd PzA

Bryansk

3rd A

Oryol

63rd A

Army Group Center (Kluge)

9th A (Model)

Yelets

Lipetsk

48th A

Livny

70th A

13th A

Sevsk

65th A

2nd TA

Kastornoye

Reserve Front (Steppe) (Konev)

Voronezh

2nd A

Seym

60th A

Kursk

Central Front (Rokossovsky)

27th A

47th A

New railroad junction

Voronezh Front (Vatutin)

Oboyan'

Stary Oskol

53rd A

5th GA

38th A

Liski

40th A

1st TA

6th GA

69th A

5th GTA

Korocha

Novy Oskol

Psyol River

4th PzA (Hoth)

Belgorod

7th GA

Oskol River

Rossosh'

Army Group South (Manstein)

Khar'kov

Army Detachment Kempf

57th A

Southwestern Front (Malinovsky)

Poltava

Donets River

Map by Dimitra Mitsou / *PERISCOPIO PUBLICATIONS*

Don River

to Moscow   Tula

The German plan of attack on the Kursk salient

Frontline 4 July 1943

Inter-front boundaries

Inter-Army Groups boundaries

Railroad line

A: Army
PzA: Panzer Army
TA: Tank Army
GTA: Guards Tank Army
GA: Guards Army

0 20 40 60 80 100 120 140 160 km

battalions), the 7th Infantry Division (Lieutenant General Fritz-Georg von Rappard, with nine battalions), the 258th Infantry Division (Lieutenant General Hans-Kurt Höcker, with seven battalions), and the 102nd Infantry Division (Major General Otto Hitzfeld, with six battalions). The neighboring XX Corps (General Rudolf Freiherr von Roman) was even weaker than the XLVI Panzer Corps as the operational plan showed no active part for it in the schedule. It fielded the 45th Infantry Division (Lieutenant General Hans Freiherr von Falkenstein, with six battalions), the 72nd Infantry Division (Lieutenant General Philipp Müller-Gebhard, with six battalions), and the 137th Infantry Division (Lieutenant General Hans Kamecke, with six battalions). The 9th Army retained a strong reserve of the 36th Infantry Division, however: Major General Hans-Karl Freiherr von Esebeck's Esebeck Battle Group (4th and 12th Panzer Divisions and the 10th Panzer Grenadier Division). Model also had the independent 21st Panzer Brigade (Panzer-Brigade) with 45 Tigers and 39 tanks of other types.

Each of the seven divisions of the German 2nd Army on the other flank had a number of infantry battalions fluctuating between four (323rd Infantry Division) and eight (327th Infantry Division). They would act as the "anvil" on which the Red Army would be crushed in the Kursk salient. Finally, all artillery batteries had three instead of four guns.

Without doubt, the most powerful German Army in the Kursk area was Manstein's 4th Panzer Army, with three corps and a total of five panzer divisions, four panzer grenadier divisions, and four infantry divisions. The weak LII Corps (General Eugen Ott) fielded the 255th Infantry Division (Lieutenant General Walter Poppe,

with six battalions) and the 332nd Infantry Division (Lieutenant General Hans Schäfer, with nine battalions) in the first line. On the other hand, the powerful XLVIII Panzer Corps of General Otto von Knobelsdorff arrayed its élite 3rd Panzer Division (Lieutenant General Franz Westhoven, with 102 tanks), the 11th Panzer Division (Major General Johann Mickl, with 118 tanks), the strongest Panzer Grenadier Division *Grossdeutschland* (Lieutenant General Walter Hörnlein, with 136 tanks, of which 13 were Tigers and 46 Panthers, 45 PzKpfw IV and 35 Assault Guns), and the 167th Infantry Division (Lieutenant General Wolf Trierenberg, with nine battalions). The 10th Panzer Brigade (51st and 52nd Panzer Battalions with 200 brand new Panthers), and the 911th Assault Gun Battalion were among the units attached to the Army.

Even stronger was the II SS Panzer Corps (Waffen-SS General Paul Hausser) which fielded the most élite of "Himmler's Private Army" divisions, indeed of the whole German military. Its troops were élite veterans and, according to Hitler, they personified the historical successors to the Teutonic Knights, as they were imbued with National Socialist ideals. The 1st SS Panzer Grenadier Division *Leibstandarte Adolf Hitler* (Major General Theodor Wisch) was positioned on the left, equipped with 145 tanks (13 of which were Tigers) and 34 assault guns, among other equipment. The 2nd SS Panzer Grenadier Division *Das Reich* (Major General Walter Krüger), with 163 tanks (including 14 Tigers) and 34 assault guns, would operate in the center. On the right would be the 3rd SS Panzer Grenadier Division *Totenkopf* (Major General Hermann Priess) with 148 tanks (15 Tigers) and 35 Assault Guns. The SS divisions and the *Grossdeutschland* Division each had six

Possessing precise information about the intentions and plans of their opponent, the Soviets lay in wait for the enemy full of self-confidence and an unshaken faith in victory.

panzer grenadier battalions, in contrast to the four in the panzer divisions of the time.

In addition, the three corps of Army Detachment Kempf (named after its General Officer Commanding the Group, Werner Kempf) would take part in the attack, southeast of the 4th Panzer Army. The III Panzer Corps (General Hermann Breith) with the 168th Infantry Division (Major General Walter Chales de Beaulieu, with nine battalions), the 6th Panzer Division (Major General Walther von Hünersdorff, with 124 tanks), the 19th Panzer Division (Lieutenant General Gustav Schmidt, with 90 tanks), and the 7th Panzer Division (Lieutenant General Hans Freiherr von Funck, with 112 tanks). The 228th Assault Gun Battalion and the 503rd Heavy Tank Battalion (with 48 Tigers) were organic to the detachment. The XI Corps (General Erhard Raus) covered the

flanks of the III Panzer Corps more to the south. It was composed of the 106th Infantry Division (Lieutenant General Werner Forst, with nine battalions), and the 320th Infantry Division (Major General Georg Postel, also with nine battalions). Kempf's third corps (XLII commanded by General Franz Mattenklott, with three infantry divisions) was in the south and, according to plans, it was to act in support of Operation "Zitadelle," but not get directly involved.

The concentration of strength, from the *Wehrmacht's* point of view, was tremendous. Its best generals, almost 900,000 of its most battle-hardened and experienced troops, 2,600 tanks and self-propelled guns, 10,000 guns and mortars, and 1,800 aircraft would strike at the enemy. If this unprecedented volume of panzers was unable to beat the Soviets, then nothing in the world could.

American medium tank M3A5 Lee in Soviet colors, 5th Guards Tank Army, Kursk, July 1943. This Lend-Lease tank was armed with a 75mm gun, a 37mm gun, and two .30cal machine guns. It had a combat weight of 28.6 tons, a speed of 26mph (41.8km/h), and carried a six-man crew. In general, the M3 tank was unpopular with the Russians. Its large silhouette, extremely poor performance on Russian roads, relatively weak engine (only 340hp while T-34-76 had 450hp engine), and sensitivity to irregularities in fuel and oil already were no great delight for Soviet crewmen, but its most important drawback was its rubber-metal tracks. During battle the rubber would burn out and tracks collapsed, immobilizing the tank. The Russian crews dubbed the American tank "a grave for six brothers." The commander of the 134th Tank Regiment wrote in one official report: "The American tanks work extremely badly in sand: their tracks are continuously falling off, the tanks sink in the sand, and then create the problem of having to move them. Because the 75mm gun is mounted in a sponson rather than in a turret, we are forced to turn the whole tank to the left or right to make a shot, and this causes the vehicle to sink deeper and deeper in the sand, causing yet more and more problems when firing and maneuvering." It is finished in Dark Olive Green. (Illustration by Dimitris Hadoulas/Historical Notes by Stelios Demiras)

Stavka Decides to Wait

If the Germans had been aware that the Soviets had managed to learn about all aspects of Operation "Zitadelle" they would not have risked attacking Kursk, notwithstanding the forces assembled for the operation. After the war it became known that *Stavka* was receiving detailed reports, thanks to its "Lucy" spy ring in Switzerland and the ring coordinator, Rudolf Roessler, who became the subject of many studies. Roessler's sources were never revealed, however, and it is still not known if there really was a traitor in the Führer's close circle (code name Werther) or if the British had simply concocted a method of occasionally leaking to Stalin secret information they had gathered through "Ultra" code-breaking intelligence.

Hitler was looking forward to taking the offensive initiative again, while Stalin was worried about losing the strategic advantage he had painfully gained at the Battle of Stalingrad. There is little doubt that Hitler knew of Stalin's impulsive temperament and, probably, kept on postponing "Zitadelle" in the secret hope that the Soviets would attack first, in which case the *Wehrmacht* could decimate them with a well-planned

**PRIVATE (*SCHÜTZE*),
KURSK 1943**
He wears the standard-issue field gray service dress (M40 tunic and trousers) and M1939 Jackboots (marching boots). Of special note are the *Heer* (Army) *Splinter Pattern Smock* and *Heer Splinter* Helmet Cover of the M1942 type. He is armed with the 7.92mm Karabiner Kar 98K carbine. The Kar 98K was adopted as the standard bolt-action rifle for the new *Wehrmacht* in 1935. It was produced by the millions in a number of factories, and production continued until the end of the war. He carries a *splinter Zeltbahn*, breadbag, canteen, mess tin, entrenching tool bayonet M1898 and stick grenades M1929. (Illustration by Johnny Shumate / Historical Notes-Comments by Stelios Demiras)

German 1st SS Panzer Grenadier Division *Das Reich* StuG III assault guns and SdKfz 251 half-tracks charge headlong during the first day of the Battle of Kursk.

counterattack. *Stavka*, however, was not going to satisfy this wish.

In the meantime, a great debate had started in March within the top Soviet military leadership about the army's next moves. Some of those who thought that the Red Army should strike first argued that German attacks had succeeded in breaking through the Soviet defenses for two consecutive summers and, on each occasion it had taken months to wear down the panzers' strength. Other proponents of a first strike cited purely psychological considerations, saying that an aggressive spirit had swept the Soviet army following the victory at Stalingrad and this should not be frittered away. The skeptics, on the other hand, reminded everybody of the Red Army's attempt to counterattack in the summer of 1942 and of how costly that had been, raising a real danger of the front's total collapse. They pointed to the tactics followed by the British at El Alamein in October 1942. There the British waited for their opponent to strike first, then wore him out, and only at that point did they counterattack. This approach was resoundingly successful, although the British had the advantage of far outnumbering Rommel in all fields.

Among the skeptics was Field Marshal Zhukov, the victor of the Battles of Moscow and Stalingrad, who had toured the Kursk front. On 8 April 1943, he submitted a written report to Stalin, stating that he was absolutely confident that the enemy would attack towards that direction and that the Red Army should concentrate its reserves at that point in order to face him. The report ended: "I consider it inexpedient for our troops to launch a preemptive offensive in the near future. It would be better for us to wear down the enemy on our defenses, knock out his tanks, then bring in fresh reserves and finish off his main grouping with a general offensive." Zhukov was determined to force the Germans to fight in a sector he chose and according to his own rules. He met the Chief of the General Staff, Field Marshal Aleksandr Vasilevsky, at the Voronezh Front headquarters two days later and found him in absolute agreement with this waiting tactic. The two field marshals had immediately and jointly decided on an operational order, to the effect that defensive measures should be taken in the salient and for the forming of a Reserve Front east of Kursk. The operational order was then forwarded to Stalin, who requested a more detailed briefing on the *Stavka's* intentions. Then during the night of 12 April, Zhukov, Vasilevsky, and Aleksey Innokentyevich Antonov (Deputy Chief of the General Staff) briefed Stalin on their plans with the help of specially prepared maps. Zhukov later wrote: "Stalin listened to what we said with an attention not seen before." Further meetings and exhaustive analyses by the staff officers were still required, however, before the Soviet leader was finally persuaded in mid-May that it was preferable that he should not attack first.

The town of Kursk, destroyed by the Germans during their retreat, was first mentioned in historical records in 1032 AD. With a population of 120,000, it dominated a purely agricultural area of flat lands and rolling hills and was one of the major communication hubs at the time. There were no major obstacles, except the Rivers Donets and Psyol, as well as the smaller Seym, Pena, and Vorskla rivers, which cut this vast area vertically. The almost flat hills and the endless fields, where the grain stood at the height of a man and the sunflowers turned gold in the sun, were an ideal operational terrain for armor, although some terrain features hindered off-road movement. The villages of this fertile place possessed pastoral names, reflecting the pre-war peace of the area. *Stavka* realized early on that the terrain did not lend itself to repulsing a large mass of armor, so it immediately engaged itself in reorganizing it. The Red Army would construct a terrible killing zone where nature had created but few obstacles.

Working day and night with the wholehearted help of the local population, the Soviet troops dug thousands of kilometers of trenches (one Soviet historian wrote that their total length was the distance between San Francisco and Montreal in Canada), set up barbed wire across a total length of 880km, laid more than a million mines (anti-tank and anti-personnel), and carved an incredible labyrinth of firing positions,

observation points and concealed outposts into the landscape. The "fire brigade team" of Field Marshals Zhukov and Vasilevsky personally supervised the construction of eight successive defense lines, each 5-6km long, which gave the defensive layout an unprecedented depth, as well as great flexibility. The reason for forming such a defense, instead of positioning all available forces in the first line, was the fact that if the Soviets amassed all their forces on a narrow front, they would simply be offering first-class targets to the Germans' 10,000 artillery pieces.

Stavka's plan was magnificent in its simplicity. Its first priority was to fight the German panzers and it provided for a defense in depth whereby, with the constant support of artillery, the panzers would be separated from the accompanying infantry. Minefields would help channel the German armor into "death zones," where artillery and strong counterattacks would destroy them. The Soviet reserves would then counterattack, striking the German salients in Oryol and Belgorod. In summary, the plan provided for checking the panzer advance, decimating the tanks in the rambling fortifications of the Kursk area, and destroying the *Wehrmacht* forces in half of the Eastern Front.

Soviet tactics were also simple. Anti-tank guns were positioned at critical points, divided into small teams of 10 apiece, with orders to shoot at the enemy tanks using converging fire. For its part, artillery would constantly hammer, pin down, and slow the advance of the German infantry.

Soviets fire a 120mm mortar. The Red Army's superiority in heavy infantry weapons and artillery was one of the most decisive factors in their victory at Kursk. They fired printed propaganda leaflets at the 3rd Panzer Division positions during the final phases of the battle: "We know you are especially fine fighters, and that one in two of you carries the Iron Cross. However, one in two of our troops carries a mortar."

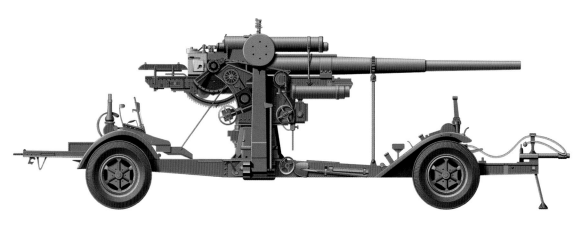

The German 8.8cm Flak 18 field gun, arguably, the most famous artillery piece of World War II. Designed as an anti-aircraft gun, the 8.8cm was also used, with great success, as an anti-tank gun and as main tank armament. It was designed by the Krupp Company in cooperation with the Bofors Company of Sweden, as the Treaty of Versailles imposed stringent restrictions on German weaponry. The gun's capabilities in the anti-tank role quickly became apparent and, on all fronts, it was feared by Allied tank crews. The gun shown here is mounted on a *Sonderhanger* 201 carriage. It was usually towed by the SdKfz 7 half-track. It is uniformly finished in Sand. (Illustration by Dimitris Hadoulas/ Historical Notes by Stelios Demiras)

Meanwhile, the Soviet troops would remain covered in their trenches and allow the panzers pass over them. Then they would suddenly appear to decimate the infantry accompanying the tanks. The panzers would, finally, be destroyed by the numerous tank destroyer regiments, by the SU assault guns, and the KV and T-34 tanks.

The Red Army's Concentration

On the Soviet side, two major fronts were going to bear the brunt of the defensive battle, while their neighboring major formations (the Western Front under General Vasily Danilovich Sokolovsky, the Bryansk Front under General Markian Mikhaylovich Popov, and the Southwestern Front under General Rodion Yakovlevich Malinovsky) would strike powerfully to the fore when the *Wehrmacht* had exhausted the power of its own attack. In order to make it impossible for the enemy to breach the front, the Soviets made use of 500,000 railroad cars to pump men and material into the area during the three-month respite.

Stavka estimated that the Central Front in the north under General Konstantin Konstantinovich Rokossovsky would bear the main German blow and that it had to be

reinforced with any means available in order to stand the test. This Front fielded six Armies and was supported by the 1,000 aircraft of Lieutenant General Sergey Ignatyevich Rudenko's 16th Air Army.

The 13th Army (Lieutenant General Nikolay Pukhov) was fresh and at full strength, after having been engaged in attack operations briefly for 12 days during February. It consisted of 11 rifle divisions, one tank brigade, five tank regiments, two anti-aircraft divisions, an artillery corps (with three divisions), and many other elements. The tremendous firepower of the 13th Army can be realized by the fact that a typical artillery division had one hundred and eight 120mm mortars, sixty-eight 76mm guns, sixty-nine 122mm howitzers, twenty 152mm guns, fifty-five 152mm howitzers and twenty-four 203mm howitzers, a force capable of checking even the strongest enemy assault. The 48th Army (Lieutenant General Prokofy Romanenko) was arrayed to its right. It had also come out intact from recent operations and possessed seven rifle divisions, four tank regiments with 134 tanks, three assault gun regiments with 44 SUs, one tank destroyer brigade and one tank destroyer regiment, one anti-aircraft division and a host of smaller units.

The newly-formed 70th Army (Lieutenant General Ivan Galanin) was

SS-OBERSCHÜTZE (PRIVATE 1st CLASS),
1st SS PANZER GRENADIER DIVISION
LEIBSTANDARTE ADOLF HITLER (LAH),
II SS PANZER CORPS, 4TH PANZER ARMY,
ARMY GROUP SOUTH, KURSK 1943
He wears the standard-issue field gray service
dress (M40 tunic and trousers) and M1939
Jackboots (marching boots). Of special note are
the Waffen-SS M42 Helmet Cover, Type-I and
the SS Smock, Type II, Oak A. He is armed with
the 7.92mm Karabiner Kar 98K carbine with
Zeiss telescopic sight. He carries M1939 leather
infantry support straps and leather man's belt,
bread bag, M1931 mess kit, entrenching
tool and bayonet M1898. (Illustration by
Johnny Shumate / Historical Notes-
Comments by Stelios Demiras)

In July 1943, the Soviets, in their deep trenches, fought with indomitable courage, preferring to die rather than surrender.

positioned to the left of the 13th Army to protect the flanks of the 65th Army that had occupied the area of Kursk in February 1943. It also fielded seven rifle divisions, one tank brigade and four tank regiments with a total of over 125 tanks, one tank destroyer division with over 100 anti-tank guns, one anti-aircraft division and the entire 1st Guards Artillery Division. The 65th Army (Lieutenant General Pavel Batov) was to the west, with nine rifle divisions, four tank regiments and one tank destroyer regiment. The 60th Army (Lieutenant General Ivan Chernyakhovsky), with four rifle divisions and one tank brigade, would have a secondary role during operations and was used as a reserve from which Rokossovsky could draw forces to strengthen his armies that would be in the thick of the battle.

While these five armies manned the first line of the northern face of the salient, other formations were kept as reserves a little further from the frontline. The major formation was the 2nd Tank Army (Lieutenant General Aleksey Rodin) with the 3rd and 16th Tank Corps and other smaller support units. Though not especially strong, it

possessed 452 tanks, 50 SUs and 12 mechanized infantry battalions making it equivalent to three panzer divisions. In addition, the Central Front was assigned the 9th and 19th Tank Corps with a total of 387 tanks and the Front's total tank strength was 1,994. Its reserve was two tank destroyer brigades, two old-style tank destroyer brigades and two independent tank destroyer regiments with a total of 360 guns, supplemented by one SU regiment. Its organic artillery included an artillery brigade, an anti-aircraft division and many rocket artillery units. Under his command, Rokossovsky had a total of 711,575 men and 11,322 guns, and rocket launchers of every type.

In a strange way, the Voronezh Front of General Nikolay Vatutin, covering the southern face of the salient, was not as heavily equipped as Pukhov's 13th Army, although it was arrayed at the point where the enemy blow was expected to materialize. Vatutin trusted the critical areas to two heroic but exhausted armies that had received the honorific title of Guards Armies and distinguished themselves during the epic Battle of Stalingrad. The 6th Guards Army (formerly 21st Army) under Lieutenant General Ivan Chistyakov, had many veterans in its ranks but also many new recruits, a fact that created cohesion problems. It was composed of seven rifle divisions, one tank brigade and two tank regiments, two artillery brigades, 15 tank destroyer regiments with 300 guns (an amazing number, considering that two of these regiments would be enough to drive back an entire panzer division), one SU regiment, four multiple rocket launcher regiments, one anti-aircraft division, and smaller units. The 7th Guards Army (formerly 64th Army) under Lieutenant General Mikhail Shumilov, also arrayed seven rifle

The Battle of Kursk was, without doubt, the swansong of the panzers, as they were never to recover from the losses and the shock sustained.

divisions, two tank brigades and three independent tank regiments, two SU regiments, four tank destroyer regiments, one anti-aircraft division, and small artillery units.

The 38th Army (Lieutenant General Nikandr Chibisov) was to the west with six rifle divisions, one tank brigade and two tank regiments, an anti-aircraft regiment and other artillery elements. The 40th Army (Lieutenant General Kirill Moskalenko), also to the west, was composed of seven rifle divisions, one tank brigade and two tank regiments, nine tank destroyer regiments with a total of 180 guns, four multiple rocket launcher regiments, one anti-aircraft division and many other artillery elements. Vatutin retained the 69th Army (Lieutenant General Vasily Kryuchenkin) as reserves. This Army fielded five rifle divisions, small artillery units but no tanks. He was careful enough also to place the powerful 1st Tank Army (Lieutenant General Mikhail Katukov) in the reserves with the 6th and 31st Tank Corps and the 3rd Mechanized Corps with a total of 542 tanks and 20 mechanized infantry battalions. Vatutin positioned the 1st Tank Army on the road to Oboyan'

and concentrated his reserves, which included the 369 tanks of the 2nd and 5th Tank Corps, in its rear. The Voronezh Front had a total strength of 625,591 men, 8,990 guns and rocket launchers, and 1,699 armored vehicles and was supported by the 900 aircraft of Lieutenant General Stepan Akimovich Krasovsky's 2nd Air Army.

The Germans planned to throw in almost all their might, but *Stavka* had the luxury of retaining strong local reserves equivalent to an entire front, under the guise of Steppe Military District that was renamed the Steppe Front on 9 July. Its Commander-in-Chief was the energetic General Ivan Konev and the front was arrayed in the triangle of Livny-Stary Oskol-Korocha. The iron fist of this reserve was none other than the 5th Guards Tank Army (Lieutenant General Pavel Alekseyevich Rotmistrov) with the 29th Guards Tank Corps and the 5th Guards Mechanized Corps. The 7th Guards Cavalry Corps and the 3rd Guards Mechanized Corps – the equivalent of the strength of another tank army – were positioned behind Rotmistrov's army. Another three independent corps (10th Tank, 1st Mechanized, and 4th Guards Tank,) equivalent to a third strong tank army, were arrayed north of the 5th Guards Tank Army and east of Voronezh. Three more mobile corps (3rd and 5th Cavalry and 2nd Mechanized) equipped with tanks were an additional reserve for the Steppe Front.

The rest of the phantom-front forces, which the German intelligence failed to identify and pinpoint, were the 5th Guards Army (Lieutenant General Aleksey Zhadov), the 27th Army (Lieutenant General Sergey Trofimenko), the 47th Army (Lieutenant General Pyotr Kozlov), and the 53rd Army (Lieutenant General Ivan Managarov). In the east, the Konev Front was lying in wait with 573,195 men, 8,510 guns and rocket launchers, and 1,639 armored vehicles. In case these forces were not able to crush the German attack, *Stavka* was ready to throw four more reserve armies (the 3rd, 11th, 52nd, and 68th) into the battle. These were held intact to the east, just in case.

Stavka did not content itself with just amassing all these impressive forces. It made serious efforts to train units during the period of respite, to equip them better with clothing and personal effects, to raise the troops' morale with lectures, talks, personal

awards, and by showing films of the German atrocities in the occupied territories of the USSR, following to the letter Napoleon's maxim "in war, psychological factors are superior to the material ones by 3 to 1." *Stavka* thus not only steeled the Soviet soldiers' will to throw the "German beast" out of their country, but also aroused their fanaticism about exacting revenge in the names of the victims. "Ivan," the subject of the Germans' mockery until then, was now ready to crush them. The majority of the tankers were mounted on the excellent T-34/76, their beloved *tridtsat'chetvyorka* or "thirty-four," as the tank was called by its crews. With a weight of 32 tons, four crewmen, a low profile, sloped armor, Christie-type suspension, a long 76.2mm gun with 77 rounds of ammunition, and a power-to-weight-ratio of 16.2hp/t, the T-34/76 was a lethal opponent, especially at distances less than 1,000m. Where the Soviets were indeed superior was in artillery, the "red god of war," as Stalin called it, which could wear down the morale of the most determined enemy. The density of artillery units was such that artillery regiments in the field outnumbered infantry regiments 3 to 2.

Russian T-60 Model 1942 light tank, 2nd Tank Army, Kursk, July 1943. The T-60 was armed with a 20mm (0.78in) gun and one 7.62mm (0.3in) machine gun. Its armor was up to 20mm (0.78in) and its weight 5.07 tons. In the Battle of Kursk the T-60s and T-70s were obsolete and the remaining tanks were withdrawn from the first line battles. It is finished in Dark Olive Green. (Illustration by Dimitris Hadoulas/ Historical Notes by Stelios Demiras)

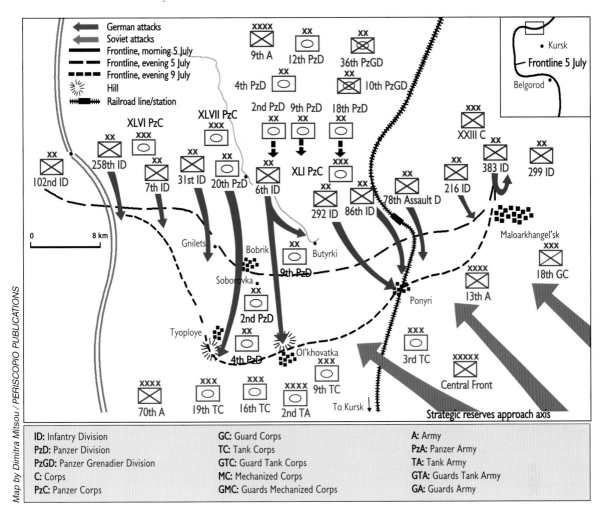

Map by Dimitra Mitsou / PERISCOPIO PUBLICATIONS

ID: Infantry Division
PzD: Panzer Division
PzGD: Panzer Grenadier Division
C: Corps
PzC: Panzer Corps

GC: Guard Corps
TC: Tank Corps
GTC: Guard Tank Corps
MC: Mechanized Corps
GMC: Guards Mechanized Corps

A: Army
PzA: Panzer Army
TA: Tank Army
GTA: Guards Tank Army
GA: Guards Army

Hitler would follow the development of the battle from his *"Wolfsschanze"* or "Wolf's Lair" headquarters in Rastenburg, East Prussia, where he was wont to follow developments in on his Eastern Front. The Führer arrived at the "Wolf's Lair" on 1 July 1943 and set about imploring his generals once more to triumph and "to dispel the gloom of our allies and crush any silent hopes still stirring within our subjugated peoples' breasts." He issued a proclamation to the troops on the eve of the battle, "Soldiers of the Reich! You are about to take part in an attack of such importance that the future of the war may hang on its outcome. Your victory will prove to the entire world, more

than anything else, that resisting the German Army has absolutely no meaning."

5 July 1943: The Lightning

In the end, Model and Manstein used different tactics in trying to discover a way to breach the Soviet defense lines. Model decided to use his infantry to achieve the initial breach and then to channel the panzers through it, exactly as Montgomery had done at El Alamein. On the other hand, Manstein and Hoth planned to use the panzers as the hammer to breach the enemy positions, by sending them to battle during the initial phase,

Model's attack in the northern part of the salient only managed temporarily to threaten the Soviet 70th Army in the Tyoploye – Ol'khovatka arc, while the attack against the Soviet 13th Army was a resounding failure.

Battlefield experience dashed the hopes that the Germans had pinned on the firepower of the new Ferdinand self-propelled guns. The 65-ton steel beast proved to be helpless in the face of small infantry groups as it, at that time, was not equipped with any secondary armament, i.e., a machine gun.

using the novel *"Panzerkeil"* (armor wedge) formation, with the Tigers forming the spearhead. The infantry in the south would support the panzers and consolidate any gains.

Concerned that the information supplied by the "Lucy" spy right might be insufficient, the Soviets sent out reconnaissance patrols in order to determine the enemy's immediate intentions. On the eve of the attack, however, a Slovenian engineer defected to the Soviets and warned them that the Germans were preparing to attack early on 5 July. Confirmation of this information came just a few hours later from a German soldier of the 6th Infantry Division captured in a night skirmish. Indeed, a strange peace reigned around the salient on the night of 4 July. The Soviets knew very well, however, that it was just the calm before the storm.

The Soviets decided to make things as difficult as possible for the enemy as the time of the attack approached. Vatutin opened fire first with his heavy artillery at 22.30 on the night of 4 July, according to well-laid plans. This preventive artillery barrage lasted for hours, with Rokossovsky's artillery joining in from 02.20. The Germans, caught in the open at their launch positions, were taken by surprise and rushed to take cover, while the Soviet shells crashed to earth, rooting up trees and other debris and throwing them

into the air. Nevertheless, the Soviets had not managed to pinpoint all the enemy positions, nor their artillery batteries, which allowed the Germans, after recovering from their initial surprise, to launch their own preparatory artillery barrage at 04.40. At the same time, the minesweeping teams were struggling to clear lanes for the avenues of approach, an extremely difficult task as the ground was sown with shrapnel and metal débris from previous battles, rendering the mine detectors virtually useless. The artillery barrage continued from both sides. At first light, the Soviet Air Force tried to launch surprise attacks on *Luftwaffe* airfields, but the Germans, having been forewarned by the long-range Freya radars, quickly took off and shot down 120 enemy aircraft with very few casualties on their side.

Following some reconnaissance, Model launched his main attack at 08.30 against the left flank of the Soviet 13th Army using his 6th, 31st, 86th, and 292nd Infantry, 78th Assault, and the 20th Panzer Divisions, with Ferdinands in support. Within the first hour, the panzers, followed by infantry mounted on half-track armored vehicles, managed to overcome the dense Soviet fortification works and reach the village of Bobrik. Some time later, the officer commanding the 6th Infantry Division, Lieutenant General Grossmann, decided to use the Tigers

Soviet Field Marshal Georgy Zhukov (right) being briefed about the battle by the Commander-in-Chief, Steppe Front, General Ivan Konev (center.)

to open the road to the south, and the terrified Soviet troops heard the roar of these monsters' engines and the creak of their tracks as they advanced menacingly towards them. The 505th Heavy Tank Battalion overran Soviet positions and continued its seemingly unstoppable advance on the village of Butyrki. The 20th Panzer Division with their PzKpfw IVs, however, met resolute resistance from Soviet anti-tank guns and infantry units that fought tenaciously, even using Molotov cocktails.

Rokossovsky faced the first crisis of the battle when, as night approached, he realized that the enemy was not going to advance on Ponyri, but, more probably, towards Ol'khovatka. To counteract this move, he immediately ordered the 3rd Tank Corps to move south of Ponyri and the 9th, 16th, and 19th Tank Corps to take up positions around Ol'khovatka. The village of Ponyri was also under attack by the XLI Panzer Corps, but the Ferdinand tank hunters did not achieve the

expected results. These slow-moving behemoths very quickly became immobilized in the trenches of the Soviet positions and separated from the supporting light tanks covering their flanks. Without defensive machine-guns, they fell victim to the Soviet troops who, having regained their courage, climbed on the German vehicles and set them ablaze by aiming their flamethrowers into the engine hatches.

Despite such minor setbacks, Model's attack kept up its pace, crushing large areas of the Soviet defensive array. Model's target was the Ol'khovatka heights. From there, the road to Kursk was downhill, both literally and metaphorically. The Germans in the 292nd Division sector discovered, to their surprise, that the Soviet infantry were not panicked in the least by the appearance of the six Ferdinands that were supporting the attack; the Russian riflemen opened fire after the steel monsters had bypassed them. The XXIII Corps also met with stiff resistance at Maloarkhangel'sk, being fiercely counterattacked as soon as it gained an inch. Model was well aware that the position had to be captured as soon as possible, in order to secure the Army's left flank from a probable arrival of fresh Soviet reserves from the east. Model's fears about the density of the Soviet trenches were confirmed as he watched hundreds of his troops fall into them.

In the south, at 05.00, the 4th Panzer Army fell with all its might onto the 6th Guards Army, having bombarded it first with artillery and 2,500 bombs dropped by the *Luftwaffe*. The 3rd Panzer Division captured the village of Butovo and, with the help of the *Grossdeutschland*, the division breached the first Soviet line of defense at 07.10, driving its defenders back towards Cherkaskoye. An ominous beginning lay in wait for the ambitious 10th Panzer Brigade. Many of its Panthers broke down before passing the front line, while the rest were trapped in an unmarked minefield. The result was that 36 of the new tanks were destroyed. The 6th Guards Army fought bravely and launched counterattacks, but Cherkaskoye eventually fell during the evening. The 11th Panzer and the 167th Infantry Divisions also gained some ground at Beryozovka, where they had breached the first line of defense with the support of the anti-tank Stukas that hit the Soviet armor with their 37mm guns.

The II SS Panzer Corps in the east was more successful, striking the weak Soviet division covering the Belgorod-Prokhorovka-Kursk railroad axis with all the might of its three divisions. The fanatical SS, with many "aces" in its ranks, opened the way, pulverizing the Soviet defenses with devastatingly accurate long-distance fire, forcing the Soviets to give ground and to fall back towards the Donets.

Soviet artillery checked the SS advance but the *Leibstandarte* managed to breach the first line of defense. During the afternoon, the *Das Reich* broke through. The Soviets redeployed a Guards division and a tank regiment in an unsuccessful attempt to check the *Leibstandarte's* advance. At the same time, the *Totenkopf*, covering the rear of the two attacking divisions, repulsed the two Soviet divisions that had been bypassed towards the Donets. The II SS Panzer Corps reported the destruction of just seven Soviet tanks, 27 anti-tank guns, 17 aircraft (a number that reveals the concerted attempts by the Soviet Air Force to check the elite German troops), and the capture of 552 prisoners. These figures show that the SS could have marked their greatest advance during the first day of "Zitadelle," although they had not yet encountered the mass of the Soviet tanks. It is generally accepted that the Soviets fought extremely tenaciously, that their anti-tank artillery had greatly improved and their tanks did not commit the errors of which they had been guilty in the past. The infantry in particular fought with an unprecedented fanaticism. "Ivan" preferred to die rather than surrender.

Army Group Kempf achieved but little success. After a fierce artillery exchange, the Germans crossed the Donets at eight points but all further attempts to move forward were met with a resolute Soviet defense. The 6th Panzer and the 168th Infantry Divisions, therefore, had to limit themselves to an advance of just 3km. The 19th Panzer Division remained stuck on the river's east bank, 19 of its 100 tanks having been knocked out by the accurate fire of the Soviet anti-tank guns. After some street fighting, the 7th Panzer Division captured

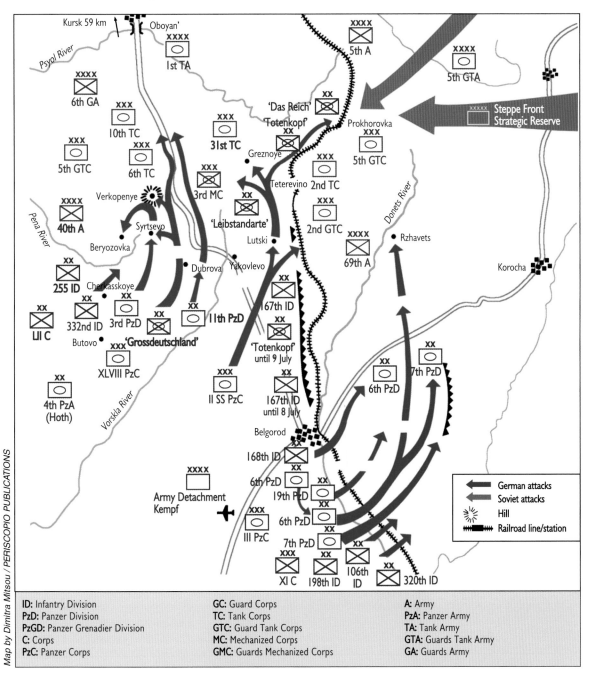

The progress made by the 4th Panzer Army during the first week of Operation "Zitadelle" was not especially impressive, but it certainly worried the *Stavka*. The Soviets were fortunate in that the Steppe Front's fresh reserves moved faster to the endangered sector than Army Detachment Kempf.

Dorogobushino and reported that, having broken through the first line of defense (the only division of the Army Detachment Kempf to achieve this during the first day of the operation), it was moving towards the second. *Stavka*

took advantage of Army Group Kempf's difficulties and moved Red Army forces into the void created between the III Panzer Corps and the II SS Panzer Corps, forcing the *Totenkopf* to fight to cover Hausser's flank instead of reinforcing the spearhead of its advance.

The first day of the operation ended in a small victory for the Germans (supported by 1,958 *Luftwaffe* sorties), although very little had been achieved with respect to encircling the Soviet troops. If the German goal was to close the trap at Kursk before Soviet reserves were able to intervene, they would have to breach at least one defense line per day, a goal that very few divisions had managed to achieve by 5 July. The OKH plan was for the salient to be encircled in four days, which meant an average advance of 30km every 24 hours. To Manstein, this now appeared unattainable.

The small German gains in the south made Vatutin move the 1st Tank Army to the rear of the 6th Guards Army (which he had already reinforced with a tank destroyer brigade and two tank destroyer regiments), successfully checking the German advance towards Oboyan'. At the same time, two tank brigades of the 38th Army undertook harassing operations on the western flank of the 4th Panzer Army. *Stavka* was worried about the situation developing along the Voronezh Front and wanted to support it in order to contain the SS effort there. To do so, it moved the 2nd and 10th Tank Corps to Prokhorovka (the 2nd Corps coming from the Southwestern Front reserves) and the 5th Guards Tank Corps, with over 200 T-34, KV and Churchill tanks, to Lutski.

6 July: The Second Soviet Defense Line is Breached

Rokossovsky's counterattack, on the eve of the second day, was supported by a mighty artillery barrage and 750 armored vehicles. It forestalled a new blow by Model, but, after a long, tough battle, was itself checked by the XLVI Panzer Corps. Then, the Germans counterattacked, after engaging more panzer reserves (the 2nd, 9th, and 18th Panzer Divisions), north of Gnilets, where a narrow breach had been forced through the Soviet defenses. In any other situation, such a concentration of firepower would have easily achieved its goal, but not at Kursk. The XLI Panzer Corps destroyed 28 enemy tanks without, however, succeeding in wresting control of Ponyri. The German attempts in the areas of Maloarkhangel'sk and Soborovska were costly in terms of casualties but brought them no results. So far, the two days of battle had cost Model's 9th Army 10,000 casualties and 200 destroyed tanks.

Hoth, in the south, also had difficulties. The foremost problem confirmed the fear concerning the strength and resilience of the Soviet defense lines that took excessively long to breach, thus giving the Soviet units ample time to withdraw in good order to the next defense line. The second "headache" had to do with the disappointing debut of the Panthers. Mechanical breakdowns and engine compartment fires rendered more than 200 of these new tanks useless already by the end of 5 July. Hoth was therefore unable to rely on the effectiveness of his long guns and their 75mm rounds that were capable of penetrating 120mm thick armor at a distance of 1,000 meters.

Morning in the south began with Soviet counterattacks: the 2nd and 5th Guards Tank Corps elements bringing their might to bear. By 08.30, Hoth had succeeded in repulsing that blow and resumed his advance. The *Grossdeutschland* moved to Luchanino and came in contact with 6th Tank

The Soviet Air Force recovered from its initial misfortune from 5 July 1943 onwards. It gradually began to gain air superiority over the ensuing days, battling hard against the *Luftwaffe*. At that time, the Yak-9, seen here, was the most modern Soviet fighter type.

Army elements south of the Pena River, where it had gained a bridgehead. Heavy Soviet artillery fire checked the 3rd Panzer Division to the left of the *Grossdeutschland,* however, but to the east, the 11th Panzer Division managed to repulse Soviet units towards Dubrova and then, by the evening, broke through the second defense line in that sector, moving then to the north.

The Germans made significant progress in the II SS Panzer Corps sector. Its forces broke through the second defense line at Yakovlevo, on the road to Oboyan', at 11.30. When the heavy casualties sustained by two of the divisions in the area of Yakovlevo (where the Commanding Officer 6th Guards Army, Chistyakov, was almost captured by the enemy) was reported to Vatutin, he sent the 31st Tank Corps and 3rd Mechanized Corps elements to the breach, but the counterattacks were unable to check the *Leibstandarte*. The *Das Reich* was fighting close to Lutski and it too managed to breach the second defense line, while the *Totenkopf,* facing the Donets, was attacked by the 2nd Guards Tank Corps and other Soviet elements. The SS succeeded in advancing a further 5km at the cost of many casualties, and they reported that the Soviet troops

had fought with the same fanaticism that had now become common inside the defense lines. General Hausser reported the destruction of 90 Soviet tanks and 83 anti-tank guns, numbers that attested all too well to the destructive efficacy of the Tiger's 8.8cm gun and the protection offered by its armor to the 76.2mm guns fired at distances over 300 meters. In addition, the SS had captured 1,609 prisoners.

The Soviet Air Force, meanwhile, had begun to recover from the losses sustained during its failed raid on the first day of the operations, and there was a slow, but noticeable, reversal of the balance of air superiority in its favor. On 6 July, in reply to the *Luftwaffe's* 899 sorties, it flew 1,632.

On the ground, Kempf launched an attack with the 7th and 19th Panzer Divisions, which had evacuated their positions for the 6th Panzer Division to deploy, east of the Donets. Von Hünersdorff, the officer commanding 6th Panzer Division, crossed the river under sustained attacks by Soviet aircraft and turned north with the objective of cutting the Belgorod-Korocha road, while both the III Panzer Corps and XLII Corps managed to break through the first defense line throughout its length. This advance deeply worried Vatutin, who requested *Stavka* to assign four tank corps and additional air forces to keep the 7th Guards Army from being forced to fall back. Vasilevsky replied that no more than two corps could, at that moment, be spared and they would arrive in the area during the next day. The 5th Guards Tank Army moved to Stary Oskol at night, to be closer to the probable point where the battle would be decided, while the 10th Tank Corps deployed northeast of Prokhorovka with the 2nd Tank Corps to the south of it.

7 July: The Panzers Advance, Despite the Resistance Encountered

Wednesday, 7 July dawned sunny and warm, and the roads on the battlefield were ready for the German advance. In the north, the XLVII Panzer Corps occupied Gnilets, although the hills in the area changed hands constantly as the two protagonists mounted counterattacks throughout the day. Model engaged the 12th Panzer Division, exerting even more pressure towards Soborovka but, by heroic fighting, the Soviets checked him, losing in a number of instances 70% of the troops of the anti-tank regiments. Despite the courage exhibited by the Germans, their advance crawled forward just a few meters, as it proved impossible to penetrate Rokossovsky's second line of defense.

Kempf maintained the pressure with his III Panzer Corps, which made a 90 degree turn to the north (placing his right flank in immediate danger), the XI Corps took up a defensive stance, and the XLII Corps supported the artillery. In the meantime, the II SS

Panzer Corps continued to storm headlong toward its objective, the third Soviet defense line that ran from Oboyan' to Prokhorovka and followed the River Psyol during most of its length. The main danger the Germans would probably have to face, was in the area of the "isthmus" in the northeast, between the Rivers Psyol and Donets. That area was an excellent fording point for the Soviet armored reserves. Manstein was worried about a threat from that direction and hesitated in the pursuit of his advance towards Oboyan'. He sought to secure the "back door" of the "isthmus" by sending Hausser's SS there, leaving only the XLVIII Panzer Corps to maintain pressure towards the north. Hoth agreed, "It is preferable to get rid of the enemy at Prokhorovka before setting our push towards Kursk into motion." During the day, 82 Soviet tanks fell victim to the *Leibstandarte*, 35 to the *Das Reich*, and four to the *Totenkopf*. While this was impressive, on the other hand, the SS destroyed just 18 anti-tank guns and captured a paltry 499 prisoners.

Hoth had 700 tanks attacking at dawn on 7 July. The *Leibstandarte* and *Das Reich* were now advancing over open ground where the gunners' well honed skills were paramount. Alarmed at this charge, Vatutin issued an order to his generals, saying, "Under no condition should the Germans be allowed to achieve a breakthrough towards Oboyan'!" The 5th Tank Corps attempted to mount a counterattack against Hausser's flanks during the afternoon, but was easily repulsed. Two more tank brigades attempted to strike back although they too were unsuccessful. A little later, the 31st Tank Corps, reinforced with over 80 anti-tank guns, attempted to check the *Leibstandarte* at Ulyanovka, but was also thrown back 10km and finally fell back towards the Oboyan' road.

The Soviets' insistence on resisting at all costs increased as their casualties mounted. Nikita Sergeevich Khrushchyov, serving as a political commissar on the Voronezh Front, warned the 1st Tank Army staff: "We either hold Kursk, or the Germans take it. They've put all their bets on a single card. For them it's a matter of life and death. We have to make sure they break their necks in the attempt!" During the morning, the *Das Reich* bore the brunt of furious Soviet counterattacks close to Teterevino, including an attack by 30 T-34s of the 2nd Tank Corps), but managed to repulse them after fierce battles and many casualties. Between 13.30 and 14.00, a new Soviet armored counterattack to recapture Teterevino was crushed by the Stukas before it threatened the *Das Reich*. In the meantime, the *Totenkopf* and the 167th Infantry Division covered Hausser's exposed right flank that was becoming even more exposed as he continued his advance northwards.

Throughout 7 July, the XLVIII Panzer Corps continued with its disjointed attack towards the second Soviet defense line, attracting numerous counterattacks. Finally, by nightfall, it had managed to capture the arc between the villages Rakovo – Alekseevka –Luchanino – Syrtsev by crossing the River Pena at many points. On the other side, the *Grossdeutschland* encountered stubborn resistance from the 3rd Mechanized and the 31st Tank Corps that contested every inch of the road to Oboyan', while the Soviet 112th Tank Brigade decisively blocked Syrtsevo off, destroying six Tigers in the process. Vatutin immediately moved the 9th Anti-aircraft Division from the 40th Army to Chistyakov (proof of the *Luftwaffe's* first-rate performance until then) and assigned

General Walter Model, General Officer Commanding 9th Army, talking with his staff. His Army represented the northern sector of the German pincer.

three tank destroyer regiments and the 86th Tank Brigade to Katukov's 1st Tank Army. He was faced with the LII Corps that was slowly advancing up the Pena River with the objective of releasing elements of the 3rd Panzer Division to move forward, in addition to the suffocating pressure on von Knobelsdorff's XLVIII Panzer Corps.

The news was not good for Hoth, with *Luftwaffe* reconnaissance reporting that there was a large concentration of Soviet armor across his front, and that at least two tank corps had hurriedly occupied positions on each side of the road to Oboyan'. Endless truck columns were moving into the salient from the east, while it became clear that the goal of encircling the Soviets was becoming less attainable by the minute.

8 July: The Battles Intensify

The ideal weather conditions of the previous days continued into 8 July, although some clouds had appeared in the sky. The Germans moved three entire *Luftwaffe* groups to the north to add impetus to the 9th Army's stagnating advance. This meant that Manstein was deprived of the air support he had counted on until then.

Repeated Soviet counterattacks were beginning to cause Model to lose the initiative, however, and the added air support was aimed at reversing that trend. Manstein's panzers had not yet lost their strength and Model threw his last reserves, the 4th Panzer Division, into the fray. These fresh troops managed to reach Tyoploye in the next two days, fighting for each inch of ground on the way. Further than that, however, they were unable to advance.

The XLVIII Panzer Corps was ordered to breakthrough at all costs on the 1st Tank Army's sector and capture Oboyan', but fanatical Soviet resistance would make that task impossible. The 3rd Panzer Division was unable to drive out the 6th Tank Corps from Beryozovka, no matter how hard it tried, although the neighboring *Grossdeutschland* did achieve a breakthrough between Syrtsevo and Gremuchy and proceeded to advance unhindered towards Verkhopenye and Novosyolovka, leaving at least 95 destroyed Soviet tanks in its wake. The XLVIII Panzer Corps captured another 10km of blood-stained Russian ground, but Vatutin replied at once with his mighty artillery, making the

earth tremble from the explosions.

The German troops were terrified in that cauldron of death as the Soviet artillery sowed carnage across the steppe. Some of the soldiers literally froze, terrified by the incredible eternal hammering that turned night into day. Others shouted with all the strength they could muster in their lungs, holding on to their comrades' hands so as not to be thrown away by the shock wave of an explosion close by. Any that dared to raise their heads over their trench parapets were cut to pieces. Many soldiers close to an explosion were buried alive under tons of earth. A *Katyusha* multiple rocket launcher division could launch a hail of 3,840 rockets, totaling 230 tons, in a few minutes. A German soldier wrote to his parents, "Never before did we feel so strongly the great Soviet numerical superiority in artillery."

The 10th Tank Corps deployed to the flanks of the 3rd Panzer Division, which Soviet artillery had pinned down with its hammering. Sporadic tank fighting occurred throughout the day, with the Germans always inflicting heavier losses than those they sustained. Red Army tactics still brought the ironic smiles to the faces of the Germans. A general who fought against the Soviets commented: "their armor tactics were very simple, and were performed like precision exercises, having been pre-planned to the smallest details. Obviously, they sought to avoid acting on the personal initiative of each tank commander." The Soviet armored formations were easy prey for the German panzers when the battle became fluid, though the Germans were fewer in number. A 6th Panzer Division trooper said that: "We had a major advantage: mobility. They seemed like a buffalo herd, having no freedom of maneuver with a leopard lying in ambush at their flanks.

A Das Reich Division Tiger tank crew leader (top) observes the area around the tank through the commander's cupola periscopes.

We were the leopards!"

The Soviets remained calm and estimated that the main danger was the II SS Panzer Corps, despite the German advance and the heavy casualties they had sustained. They continued to gather reserves in order to check it. Manstein received reliable information that the 5th Tank Army and the 69th Army were moving fast to halt his advance, while the Soviet Air Force tried hard to slow down the corps' spearhead units. The SS engaged the Soviet armored formations and infantry that had been attempting to cut off Hausser's vanguard on a 15km front at Gryaznoye since that morning. When this engagement had broken off, new waves of Soviet armor, among them vehicles of the 5th Guards Tank Army – a formation that was identified for the first time by the Germans – showed up east of Teterevino and attempted to recapture it from the *Leibstandarte*. The attempt was unsuccessful, partly due to the lethal fire of First Lieutenant Bruno Meyer's Hs 129 anti-tank aircraft. At the same time, the *Das Reich* was engaged in a bloody skirmish against the 2nd Tank Corps, and was in danger of losing its entire divisional artillery at a certain point in the battle.

The SS grenadiers were also engaged in fearsome battles with the enemy and were responsible for one-third of the 183 Soviet tanks destroyed that day by their corps. They took 2,192 prisoners and destroyed 111 anti-tank guns (the equivalent of five tank destroyer regiments,) but still there was no sign of a Soviet collapse. On the contrary, although they had been defeated, they fell back to the north in good order. The German 167th Infantry Division occupied positions to cover the flanks on 8 July, releasing the *Totenkopf* to fight to the north. By this time, however, the

German infantry, supported by the MG 34 machine gun, charges to seize another Soviet position.

Totenkopf Division was weakened, with only 5 Tigers and 28 of the original 42 PzKpfw IVs remaining operational.

The III Panzer Corps (Army Detachment Kempf) also met with stiff resistance in its push to the north, while, at the same time, trying to fill the gap on the 4th Panzer Army's right. Manstein realized that he faced more Soviet forces than he had initially estimated and, without adequate reserves, abandoned the advance towards Korocha. His aim now was to coordinate Hoth and Kempf into a common axis of attack. Vatutin, however, had anticipated this change of plan and ordered the 2nd Tank Corps to disengage from the German cordon surrounding it and to fall back south of Prokhorovka in order to harass the *Das Reich*.

Stavka, as it anticipated, was always in control of the battle that developed, in spite of the success announced by the Germans. On 8 July, it decided to greatly reinforce the sorely tried 6th Guards Army and 1st Guards Tank Army by the expedient of moving the 111th Guards Artillery Regiment, the 38th and 66th Rocket Launcher Regiments, the 12th, 222nd, 438th,

The Soviet answer to the Tigers, Panthers, and Ferdinands were the SU (*Samokhodnaya Ustanovka*) series of self-propelled guns. The heaviest variant was the monstrous SU-152, armed with a 152mm gun. These armored vehicles proved an unpleasant surprise for the Germans.

869th, and 1244th Tank Destroyer Regiments, the 180th Tank Brigade, the 59th and 60th Tank Regiments, and the 4th Anti-tank Regiment into the salient. Rotmistrov's troops (the 5th Guards Tank Army) were also moving to engage the enemy and, following a 360km forced march, had deployed their main forces 10km north of Prokhorovka after nightfall. The 5th Guards Army was also reassigned from the Steppe Front to the Voronezh Front and, during the night of 8 July, it began its march to the new positions between Rotmistrov and Katukov. While the Germans might have destroyed over 500 Soviet tanks there still remained a further 1,500 deployed between their vanguards and Oboyan'. After bitter, prolonged fighting, the *Wehrmacht* had broken through two defense lines, but there were still another six lines to Kursk.

9 July: The Fatal Fight for the third Defense Line

The German advance in the south, with the exception of Army Group Kempf, had already slowed significantly, and Stalin ordered the Voronezh Front to check the enemy at all costs in order to launch the Red Army's planned great counterattack at Oryol (named Operation "Kutuzov") and Belgorod (named Operation "Rumyantsev"). Vatutin, seeking to avoid any chance of a breakthrough along his front, preferred to sacrifice mobility in order to establish strong fixed defenses. To this end, he issued orders for the 1st Tank Army to bury its tanks into hull down positions with just the turrets showing above ground, thus presenting a much smaller target to the enemy.

The II SS Panzer Corps advanced to the north and reached the River Psyol at night, having repulsed the 31st Tank Corps counterattacks on the way. The SS grenadiers consolidated the area north of Gryaznoye and gained their first bridgehead north of the Psyol River at Vesyoly. They re-established contact with the XLVIII Panzer Corps, that had advanced from the left and positioned itself strongly in Novosyolovka, but all attempts to capture Kochetovka had failed. Von Knobelsdorff's attention was elsewhere on the arc of Beryozovka-Verkhopenye-Hill 247, where the Soviet 6th Tank Corps refused to retreat, despite enduring almost overwhelming pressure by the 3rd Panzer and *Grossdeutschland* Divisions. Throughout the day, Hausser's divisions had to repulse continuous counterattacks by the 5th Mechanized and the 2nd Tank Corps with over 100 Soviet tanks taking part in a number of these assaults. To the south, the 2nd Guards Tank Corps was applying strong pressure on the 167th Infantry Division, but the Germans held their ground. The SS troops fought viciously on 9 July, inflicting, but also suffering, heavy casualties. They only managed to destroy 18 enemy tanks, revealing that the Soviets had become much more careful in the use of their armor. The capture of a mere 62 prisoners was a

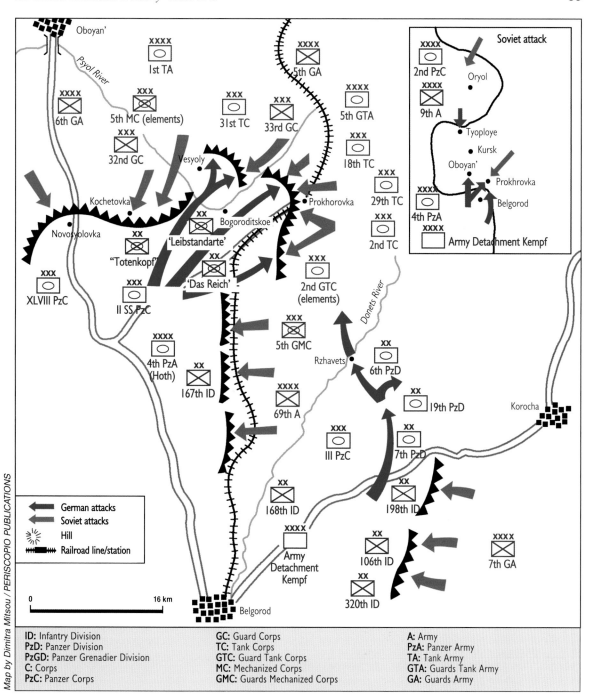

ID: Infantry Division
PzD: Panzer Division
PzGD: Panzer Grenadier Division
C: Corps
PzC: Panzer Corps

GC: Guard Corps
TC: Tank Corps
GTC: Guard Tank Corps
MC: Mechanized Corps
GMC: Guards Mechanized Corps

A: Army
PzA: Panzer Army
TA: Tank Army
GTA: Guards Tank Army
GA: Guards Army

good indication that the Voronezh Front troops were not going to "break" soon.

Meanwhile, the III Panzer Corps enjoyed greater success, managing to advance in an "armor wedge," spearheaded by the 6th Panzer Division with the 7th and 19th Panzer

The awe-inspiring tank battle at Prokhorovka on 12 July 1943 led to the culmination of the operation. The Germans were unaware that the Soviets still possessed huge reserves, and turned the II SS Panzer Corps northeast in order to block the passes between the Psyol and Donets Rivers to enable them to continue the advance to the north. In doing so, they came into contact with Pavel Rotmistrov's 850 tanks before Army Detachment Kempf's forces could cross the Donets and take part in the engagement.

The Germans also had their heroes in the Battle of Kursk. First Lieutenant Michael Wittmann (in the black uniform), a Tiger tank commander of the *Leibstandarte*, destroyed 28 Soviet tanks and the same number of anti-tank guns during Operation "Zitadelle." A large part of his success was due to his gunner, Balthazar (Bobby) Woll (right), who could hit a target even while the tank was on the move.

Divisions on its flanks, and crossing the Belgorod-Korocha road and moving north. The other corps of the Army Detachment Kempf remained static, realizing that the main action was now in the north and not in the east.

The situation was not favorable for the Germans. Manstein saw on his battle maps that the advance was slowing down dramatically and that more forces were now needed for the operation to regain its lost momentum. He assigned the *Totenkopf* to spearhead the attack, which brought some relief, although it was not enough to break the Soviet armor's steel cordon. The German field marshal issued orders to the 1st Panzer Army, which was holding the front to the south of the River Mius, urgently to send its XXIV Panzer Corps (23rd Panzer Division and 5th SS Panzer Grenadier Division *Wiking*) to Kempf during the night of 9 July. This significant force would be unable to arrive at the Kursk salient before 17 July, however. In the meantime, Manstein had not yet lost hope that Hausser's élite forces would finally manage to open the road to Prokhorovka with the *Leibstandarte* and the *Das Reich* moving on the two sides of the railroad line and the *Totenkopf* following their moves from the north banks of the Psyol River.

10-11 July: The Weather turns against the Germans

What Manstein had not anticipated was that, from the morning of 10 July, nature would turn against him. Thick clouds covered the sky and summer

rains turned the already bad Russian roads into quagmires. The cloud cover prevented the *Luftwaffe* from operating in the efficient manner for which it had become known, and the II SS Panzer Corps managed, on average, to gain just 5km, struggling through the mud. The *Leibstandarte* and the *Totenkopf* reported the destruction of just two Soviet tanks, while the *Das Reich* reported 97 tanks and 26 anti-tank guns destroyed. Bogoroditskoye, however, fell to the SS, including the capture of 245 prisoners, and the unceasing Soviet counterattacks were thrown back. The II Panzer Corps to the south advanced deeper, threatening the Donets, as Soviet pressure was noticeably less than on the previous day. The XLVIII Panzer Corps spent most of its time repulsing Soviet counterattacks that were mounted in waves, and the LII Corps reported that it had, finally, completed the elimination of the largest proportion of the 6th Tank Corps and that it had fully consolidated the southern banks of the Pena.

There were meager German gains during 9 July, and Manstein was thinking of a way to destroy the Soviet 69th Army that had appeared on the flanks of the 6th Guards Army. He would have to combine the II SS Panzer and the III Panzer Corps into a fist in order to do so, but it would still be extremely difficult to achieve over the next few days. Manstein's optimism, however, had not wavered and he gave orders for the SS and Army Detachment Kempf to continue their advance during the next day. The weather, however, seemed to have struck a strange alliance with Vatutin. Storms raged throughout 11 July, and wheeled transport sank into the mud, unable to follow the tracked vehicles. Ammunition re-supply was not reaching the combat units and their

Commander-in-Chief, Voronezh Front, General Nikolay Vatutin, consults a map during the battle. Contrary to *Stavka's* initial estimates, it was Vatutin's units that finally bore the brunt of the German attack.

fighting ability plummeted. The SS engineers succeeded, by superhuman effort, in constructing a 62-ton bridge over the River Psyol at Bogoroditskoye, strong enough for the Tigers to cross, but the torrential rains prevented the *Totenkopf* from exploiting the bridgehead it had gained with such sacrifice. The *Luftwaffe* was grounded and all vehicles, except tanks, were stuck in the mud. Nevertheless, the SS divisions approached Prokhorovka, beating off stubborn Soviet resistance, destroying 72 tanks and 22 anti-tank guns and capturing 309 prisoners. The Germans' only hope of victory lay with the III Panzer Corps' headlong advance in the south.

In the north, the German 9th Army, showing a lot more zeal, continued its attempts to move deeper towards Tyoploye and Ol'khovatka, and engaging its last mobile reserve, the 10th Panzer Grenadier Division, in its endeavors. These units failed to live up to expectations, however, due to their inability to move parallel with the XLVII Panzer Corps. Faced with the possibility of a stagnating front, Kluge and Model agreed to use fresh reserves from Army Group Center the next

morning. The Red Army forestalled them, however, with its own massed attack.

12 July: Battle of the Titans in Prokhorovka

Time had now run out for the Germans. *Stavka*, calculating the delivery of its blows to perfection, was ready at 8.30 to launch the most decisive strike by throwing the entire 5th Guards Army at the II SS Panzer Corps. This mass flowed like a river of lava toward the enemy, aiming for a frontal blow. It was formed into two waves, with the first including the 2nd, 18th, and 29th Guards Tank Corps with 450 tanks and the second with the 2nd Tank and the 5th Guards Mechanized Corps with about 300 tanks. The remaining tanks were kept in reserve.

The clash of giants took place under a leaden sky, and often under torrential rain, on a stretch of flat terrain, eight square kilometers, to the west of Prokhorovka. The Germans, not realizing what the Soviets were up

The German Panther tanks were used for the first time during the Battle of Kursk, but they proved extremely unreliable as most were immobilized because of mechanical problems. Others that did manage to make contact with the enemy were destroyed during the tank battles, as was the one in this picture.

to, began their advance on Monday morning, 12 July, with the *Totenkopf* in the north, the *Leibstandarte* in the center, and the *Das Reich* south of the railroad line. The Soviets estimated that Hausser had at least 500 operational tanks that morning. The number was, apparently somewhat inflated, since the SS started Operation "Zitadelle" with just 456 tanks, 137 assault guns, and 35 Tigers. The total number of the German tanks could not have exceeded 350 on 12 July, although it is possible (but not verified) that Hausser's vanguards had been reinforced with a heavy tank battalion that could have meant an extra 60-70 Tigers.

Meanwhile, the German tank crews were exhausted after seven days of combat. Many panzers had broken down, and most of their ammunition had been used up. On the other hand, Rotmistrov had more tank crews and they were fresh, experienced, and their ammunition racks were full. Five

hundred and one of their tanks were T-34s, 264 were the light T-70s and there were also 35 British Churchills. In addition, the four regiments equipped with SU-76 self-propelled guns were a lethal threat to the Tigers. Rotmistrov was fully aware that the major tactical advantage of the panzers lay with the Tigers' ability to fire from long range and the accuracy of the German gunners, so he gave orders for his tanks to charge headlong at the enemy, giving him but the minimum of time to fire from a long range. The plan was successful and soon the German and Soviet tanks became a thundering, whirling mass, firing at each other from point-blank range, more reminiscent of a medieval battle between iron-clad knights than a 20th century confrontation. German superiority was nullified and the fight became disjointed, a series of isolated engagements, where even the light Soviet T-70s could deal a blow to the panzers. The German tanks may have had thicker armor and better guns, but there were more Soviet tanks and they had better mobility.

"We found ourselves facing an inexhaustible mass of enemy armor," a German officer later commented. "The clouds of smoke prevented the *Luftwaffe* from supporting us and quite quickly many T-34s had broken through our echelons and were wheeling around us like rats." This fierce battle, described as the largest tank battle during World War II, continued for 12 hours. Crews, locked down in their mobile steel forts suffocated in the smoke, fumes, humid air, and the stress of battle. Tanks fired, others blew up, turrets weighing many tons flew through the air, many disappearing into a hell of a fire, while other tanks crashed, mortally wounding their crews. On both sides, the air force and artillery feared to

At Kursk, the Tiger heavy tank was, without doubt, the king of the battlefield, thanks to its ability of being able to hit enemy armor with its 8.8cm gun (with a 92-round reserve) from long range while their thick armor made them almost invulnerable.

intervene in this incredible mêlée, mostly because of the danger of hitting friendly tanks.

The only thing that could help the Germans regain their balance in the unrelenting battle was the early arrival of the III Panzer Corps. General Breith, the corps' commanding officer, exhorted his men to the utmost, and his troops fought hard and courageously to push through to the area. He was, however, to be "awarded" the unenviable distinction of being the Battle of Kursk's "Emmanuel de Grouchy," as he reached the battlefield a few critical hours too late, just as the French field marshal had done at Waterloo in 1815. The 6th Panzer Division, with its 300 tanks and assault guns that could have helped Hausser win the battle, had captured an intact bridge over the Donets, thanks to the daring of Major Franz Bäke, but the III Panzer Corps was still 20km from Prokhorovka. The Soviets, however, managed to check Breith in a grueling attritional encounter, throwing 120 tanks, 20 assault guns, 32 anti-tank guns, and five mechanized infantry battalions against him, indifferent to any casualties. The *Luftwaffe* then managed to add to Breith's difficulties by mistakenly bombing the 6th Panzer Division at Rzhavets, killing 15 troops and wounding 49.

By sunset, the Germans were forced to concede that the tank battle at Prokhorovka had destroyed all their hopes for a victory in the east. Almost 300 tanks, 88 guns, and 300 other German vehicles lay in flames on the steppe together with the remnants of more than half of the Soviet 5th Guards Tank Army tanks. Both sides had given and received terrible punishment. The Germans failed to concentrate their forces in Prokhorovka early enough and it would cost them dearly. The II SS Panzer Corps reported the destruction of hundreds of enemy tanks, 44 anti-tank guns and the capture of 968 prisoners, but the 5th Guards Tank Army dominated the battlefield, where a deadly silence now reigned supreme. British historian John Erickson wrote that all around one could see: "destroyed tanks, wreckage, limbs, frying pans, artillery shells, decks of cards and pieces of bread."

Driving back the Germans in the tank battle at Prokhorovka meant, in all practicality, the end of the Battle of Kursk. After many days of continuous combat and heavy casualties, the

A Soviet tank crew inspects the turret of a destroyed Tiger and their faces reveal their satisfaction. The heavy German tank could stand many hits from enemy rounds thanks to its thick armor, but a 76.2mm round fired by a T-34 could penetrate it from close range.

panzer units were too exhausted to score any noteworthy success. The Soviet Operation "Kutuzov," launched by the Western and the Bryansk Fronts, fell like a storm onto the 2nd Panzer Army that was covering the Oryol area and the Soviets achieved an immediate breakthrough. The Germans would not only be unable to reinforce the 9th Army, but the Army would have to disengage and support the operations around Oryol. On 13 July, Hitler summoned Kluge and Manstein to his headquarters for a conference. He announced that the Western Allies had already landed in Sicily with 160,000 men and 600 tanks, and that German forces had to be sent to the Italian Front, to bolster Mussolini's dispirited army. Operation "Zitadelle" had to be broken off. Manstein argued strongly, stating that the battle had just reached a critical juncture, that his forces had destroyed all the tank corps that the Soviets had thrown against them and that it would be unfair to stop the battle now and let victory slip through the *Wehrmacht's* fingers. He begged Hitler at least, to allow the 9th Army to maintain its positions in order to pin down Rokossovsky, so that he, Manstein, could continue his advance and cut off the salient by himself. A general of the

4th Panzer Army caustically commented, "We were in the embarrassing position of a man who is holding a wolf by its ears and dare not let him go."

The Eastern Front's Balance is Reversed

Manstein, was incorrect in his assumption. The Soviets had attacked the Oryol salient with an unprecedented ferocity, throwing into the battle 1,287,600 troops on three fronts, and firing 300 railroad carloads of artillery shells into the German positions within just one hour. The situation was also equally desperate for the *Wehrmacht* in the south, where the Steppe and the Voronezh Fronts continued to exert overwhelming pressure, using 1,144,000 troops to recapture Belgorod. In addition, Von Kluge urgently needed the 9th Army to cover the breaches on his front. Despite this, Hitler gave Manstein permission to continue his attack alone.

In the Kursk salient, Tuesday, 13 July dawned with new storms, creating difficulties for the SS who were trying to regroup after the bloody losses sustained the day before. Hausser's troops continued their ferocious attack: they destroyed 144 Soviet tanks that day (although many of them were not complete losses), but then just three on Wednesday; 44 on Thursday; and finally 18 on Friday, 16 July. These operations, however, were of no use, since no ground was gained. To the east, under strong counterattacks by the 1st Soviet Tank Army, the XLVIII Panzer Corps was pinned down and struggling to save itself, while the III Panzer Corps was the only one able to continue its advance although it was forced to go the defensive for good on Saturday, 17 July. On that day, Hitler lost his temper and demanded that

Manstein immediately discontinue the attack and to send the *Grossdeutschland* to von Kluge. He was also ordered to disengage the II SS Panzer Corps, in order to send some elements of it to Italy with the remainder to be used as mobile reserves. So it was that the entire German battle array began falling back towards its launch positions and the Soviets regained ground that the Germans had won at the cost of so much blood.

The Soviets themselves admit, in spite of the often-quoted exaggerated estimates, to have lost 1,614 tanks during the Battle of Kursk. This number may be accepted as a true figure, since the Soviets had control of the battlefield and would therefore be able to recover and repair about half of their damaged vehicles. In addition, their casualty count included 46,330 men dead and missing, with a further 24,000 prisoners and 107,517 wounded. Meanwhile, the Germans maintained that their casualties did not exceed 30,000 men, but this figure is undoubtedly less than their actual losses.

The great Soviet counteroffensive soon became an avalanche. By 23 July, the Red Army had regained all the territory lost during Operation "Zitadelle" and was continuing to advance, liberating Oryol and Belgorod on 5 August 1943, and Bryansk two weeks later. Stalin ordered 12 salvoes to be fired from 124 guns and for all the church bells to toll in Moscow, in celebration of these successes. These joyful salvoes would be repeated in Moscow another 354 times before the end of the war.

"An element of tragedy colors the German defeat at Kursk," wrote the British historian Alan Clark. "Having almost reached annihilation at the gates of Moscow, having been terribly maimed at Stalingrad, the magnificent

German Army had recovered twice. Finally, equipped with new and more terrible weapons, it let every chance of a victory slip from of its hands by a tragic series of errors and bad calculations that added to the ignominious result." The confrontation at Kursk was, without doubt, the greatest armored battle in history and, possibly, the most decisive engagement of World War II. Following the defeat in this battle, the panzers, the pride of the German Army, would never regain the old glory that had led them victorious from the English Channel to the banks of the Volga River. Hitler's ability to conduct offensive operations was drastically curtailed after Kursk, while the Red Army, having gained the strategic initiative, would never let it slip from its grasp right up to the final fall of the Third Reich.

The SS Tigers advance! But, the Soviets were ready to sacrifice lives and material in order to check their progress.

Air Operations During the Battle of Kursk

On the Eastern Front, the battle of Kursk was decisive because the Soviets gained the initiative that they were never to relinquish. The merciless combat on the ground was mirrored by the equally merciless clash in the air, where hundreds of aircraft swirled in desperate dogfights. The Soviet air force managed to win the air battle, thanks to its superiority in aircraft and personnel. In addition to their superiority in aircraft numbers, the Soviets also displayed air combat skills equal to those of the German pilots, whose superiority and experience had worked in their favor during previous operations.

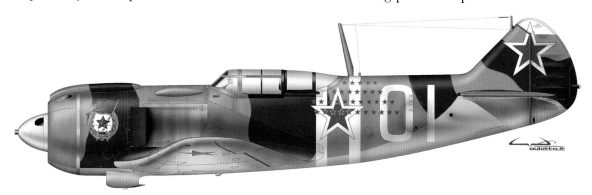

Soviet fighter Lavochkin La-5FN "White 01" flown by Capt. V. I. Popkov of the 5th GvIAP (Guards Fighter Aviation Regiment), 11th GvIAD, 2nd GvShak in 1943. Note the Guards' emblem on the engine cowling. The color scheme is Dark Gray (FS. 36187)/Medium Gray (FS. 36270) over Light Blue Gray (FS. 35414). The Lavochkin La-5 was among the most widely produced Soviet fighters of WWII. The first production planes flew in the summer of 1942 and received their baptism of fire in the Stalingrad sector fighting against the nimble Messerschmitt Bf 109F-4s and heavier Bf 109G-2s. It was soon made obvious that the type's teething problems needed attention and most were resolved in the improved La-5F version. The upgraded La-5FN appeared in the spring of 1943, powered by the uprated M-82FN powerplant. Close to the ground, the La-5FN was deemed superior in turning even to the famous Fw 190, but was at a serious disadvantage over 3,000m and had a very short range. The Soviet ace Ivan Kozhedub scored 45 of his 62 kills, flying in the La-5FN. (Illustration by Vincenzo Auletta/Historical Notes by Stelios Demiras)

Soviet fighter Lavochkin La-5FN "White 93" of the 32nd Gv.IAP, 3rd Gv.IAD, 1st Gv.IAK flown by Senior Lt. V. Orekhov during the battle of Kursk, July 1943. The color scheme is Dark Grey (FS. 36187)/Medium Gray (FS. 36270) over Light Blue Gray (FS. 35414). The spinner and the cowling are red. (Illustration by Vincenzo Auletta/Historical Notes by Stelios Demiras)

The Battle of Kursk was the third German summer operation on the Eastern Front following the June 1941 invasion. Its goal – the elimination of the Kursk salient – was, without doubt, an objective less challenging than the 1941 attack on Moscow or, for that matter, the 1942 drive towards the Caucasus oilfields. The Operation, codenamed "Zitadelle" (Citadel), had the aim of eliminating the Soviet forces in the salient by a simultaneous attack from north and south. The battle started on 5 July and culminated in the greatest tank battle of World War II, but was equally a challenge for the air forces involved.

The *Luftwaffe* assembled 1,800 – 2,000 aircraft of various types, two thirds of its available force on the entire Eastern Front, to support the operation. The *Luftwaffe's* support was not confined in the air. On the ground the Germans fielded a large number of anti-aircraft artillery units equipped with the deadly 8.8cm guns. The 1st

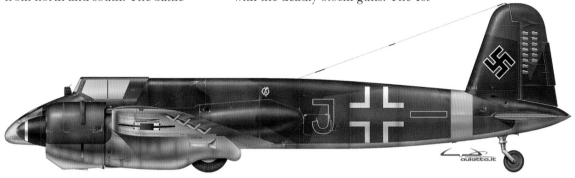

German ground-attack aircraft Henschel Hs 129B-2 *Panzerknacker* **flown by Hptm. Rudolf-Heinz Ruffer of the 10.(Pz)/SG 9 as it appeared during the battle of Kursk. He died just over a year later (on 16 July 1944) after being hit by enemy flak. Having destroyed over 70 enemy tanks, he was decorated with the Knights Cross. This plane wears the typical camouflage splinter pattern: RLM 70/71/65. The Henschel Hs 129 was a well-armored ground attack aircraft that, in its initial Argus-engined version, lacked success due to its being under-powered. The follow-on Hs 129B series used French Gnome-Rhone 14 MO4/05 engines, which were being produced in German-occupied France. The Hs 129B-1 thus became the first German plane with a French powerplant. Its flying characteristics improved, especially when taking off and landing, and the plane became much safer to maneuver close to the ground, where it was meant to operate. Although it was a capable ground attack aircraft, the Hs 129B-2 really came into its own as a dedicated anti-tank plane. The specialized Schlachtgeschwadern, made up of Hs 129s and Fw 190s, were used in large concentrations during the battle of Kursk. The Hs 129B-2 was well-armed with two 7.92mm MGs, two 20mm MG 151/20 cannon in the nose, and a 30mm MK101 (later MK103) cannon in an underslung ventral pod. The plane depicted was flown by 'ace' Rudolf-Heinz Ruffer of 8 (Pz) Sch.G1, when flying from the Kuban, during May 1943. Ruffer received the Knights Cross on 9 June 1944 when he had been credited with 72 tanks destroyed. This Henschel sports the classic RLM 70/71/65 camouflage. (Illustration by Vincenzo Auletta/Historical Notes by Stelios Demiras)**

German ground-attack aircraft Henschel Hs 129B-2 *Panzerknacker*, **Werk Number 0166, of the 8.SchG 2 as it appeared during the battle of Kursk (4 July 1943 – 23 August 1943). Anti Tank Units, such as the SchG 2, flew in support of the Panzer divisions during the greatest tank battle of the Second World War. This plane wears the typical camouflage splinter pattern: RLM 70/71/65. (Illustration by Vincenzo Auletta/Historical Notes by Stelios Demiras)**

In 1943, the Soviet fighters proved to be dangerous opponents for the *Luftwaffe*. This was predominantly due to the introduction into service of many new types, like the Lavochkin La-5FN.

Air Division (*Flieger-Division*) of the 6th Air Fleet (*Luftflotte*) was assigned to support the 9th Army in the north, flying from Oryol, Poltava, and Bryansk. The 4th Air Fleet would support the 4th Panzer Army in the south, flying from Mikoyanovka, Khar'kov, Zaporozhye, and Varvarovka. The *Luftwaffe* was to play a major role in the battle, as it had to cover for the paucity of howitzers and anti-tank guns, especially following the Stalingrad disaster.

The Soviet Central Front, supported by the 16th Air Army of Field Marshal Sergey Ignatyevich Rudenko, was positioned opposite the 9th German Army. The Voronezh Front in the south had the support of Field Marshal Stepan Akimovich Krasovsky's 2nd Air Army. The Soviets had assembled 2,800 - 3,000 aircraft but could count on more, if they needed to tap their reserves. Most of these aircraft were fighters and it was their mission to achieve air superiority over the Germans. *Stavka* had formed the Steppe Front as its reserve and the 5th Air Army was assigned to support it. Units of the 17th Air Army (under the command of the neighboring Southwestern Front) also took part in the operations. In fact, the Kursk front consumed 27 percent of available Soviet aircraft.

Soviet armor was a priority target for the *Luftwaffe*. To fulfill this mission, five squadrons were assembled on the southern flank of the salient: two were from the 1st Close Support Wing (*Schlachtgeschwader - Sch.G.* 1), two from Sch.G. 2 and the *Panzerjägerstaffel/JG51*, all equipped with the Hs 129B and based at Mikoyanovka and Varvarovka. The Battle of Kursk was an opportunity for the Henschel Hs 129B-2s to operate for the first time on such a scale on the Eastern Front. The B-2 variant was powered by two French Gnome-Rhône 14M 700 hp engines, and was armed with two MG 151/20 20mm cannons and two MG 17 7.92mm machine-guns in the nose. The B-2/R-2 version had a gun pod fitted with the MK101 30mm gun and 30 rounds. The Test Squadron 1./St.G. 2, flying the Ju 87G-1s, with the famous Hans-Ulrich Rudel as commander, was assigned to the south, supplementing the force of specialized anti-tank aircraft. The Junker Ju 87G-1 had two BK 37mm guns mounted in underwing gondolas, the weight and aerodynamic drag of which reduced the performance of the aircraft below that of other Stuka variants. Anti-tank support in the northern part of the attack was assigned to the 2nd Squadron of St.G. 2 with Ju 87G-1s, which was attached to the Dive Bomber Wing St.G. 1, at Bryansk, and the *Panzerjägerstaffel/ZG 1* equipped with the Bf 110G that was armed with large-caliber guns.

The *Luftwaffe* raided airfields, communication hubs, and troop concentrations in the salient for some time prior to the launch of the assault on Kursk. For the attack to succeed, the *Luftwaffe* had to retain air superiority and prevent the Soviet fighters from attacking the panzer columns while also protecting the vulnerable Ju 87Ds. Both the *Luftwaffe* and the Soviet Air Force continued bombing airfields and communication lines as the set date for launching the operation approached.

Seeking to destroy the German aircraft on the ground, the Soviets' 2nd Air Army, based in the southern part of the salient, launched a large number of aircraft in an attack on the major German air base at Khar'kov. The incoming attackers were detected by a long-range Freya radar, however, and Focke-Wulf Fw 190s and Messerschmitt Bf 109Gs of the JG 3 and JG 52 wings scrambled at the last moment. Around 500 aircraft engaged in fierce dogfights, with the Soviets losing 70 planes (the Germans put Soviet losses at 120). This Soviet failure and the losses they sustained left the Germans with primacy in the air.

On 5 July, the first day of the operation, the *Luftwaffe* flew 2,400 sorties in support of the 4th Panzer Army, sustaining just 19 losses. The Ju 87s began first, flying low in an attempt to destroy the forward defense lines. The successful air support allowed the II SS Panzer Corps to advance to a depth of 20km into the Soviet defense lines. The Ju 87G-1s fired at the Soviet armor, hitting the engine compartment of the tanks with devastating results. The Fw 190s added their weight by dropping SD-1 and SD-2 bombs that scattered respectively 180 or 360 fragmentation bomblets with deadly results on the howitzer crews.

The situation was even better for the Germans in the south. With *Luftwaffe* support, they succeeded in breaching the defense line covering the Belgorod-Kursk road axis by the afternoon of 6 July. The XLVIII Panzer Corps attacked the Soviet positions at Syrtsev and Yakovleno, but came under heavy air attack. The strength of the new Tiger tanks and the continuous air support they

received were a tough combination for the Soviets to crack.

The German advance on the southern face of the salient was a major threat to the Soviets. To counteract this threat, late in the evening of 7 July, the 2nd Guards Tank Corps commander was ordered to assemble his forces and attack the flanks of the II SS Panzer Corps from the west, cutting off its supply route. By chance the Soviet corps was spotted the next day by Captain Bruno Meyer flying a Henschel Hs 129 on routine patrol. In no time, Combat Group Druschel, flying Hs 129s and Fw 190s, attacked the T-34s and hit the infantry with bombs. Fifty T-34s were destroyed in an hour.

On 7 July, almost half the 4th Air Fleet strength was concentrated on the northern side of the salient to support operations in the area of Ol'khovatka. Only 1,173 sorties were flown that day, while the Soviet Air Force began to gradually increase its mission numbers. Over the following three days, both sides took great pains to assemble large numbers of tanks, artillery, and aircraft. An attack by Il'yushin Il-2M3 aircraft against the 9th Panzer Division heading for Ponyri was noted, during which the Soviets reported that 60 tanks were destroyed.

A close view of a Ju 87G-1's armament. Its two 37mm guns made it a dangerous opponent of the Soviet tanks. It was extremely vulnerable, however, if operating without top fighter cover around the target area.

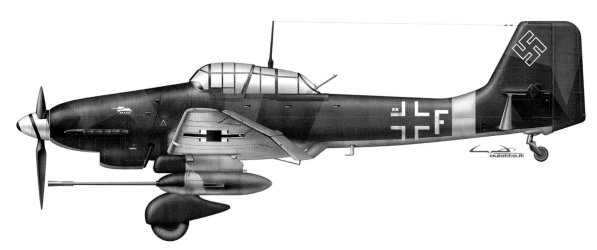

German anti-tank aircraft Junkers Ju87G-1 Stuka "Gustav the tank killer," serial F, of the Experimental Anti-Tank Tactics Section. This Unit was based at Bryansk, Russia, during Spring 1943 to study new operational tactics for anti-tank aircraft. Its "test of fire" was the Battle of Kursk. Its Ju 87s often had the undercarriage fairings removed, to allow the planes better handling on the muddy airfields. This plane wears the typical camouflage pattern for Stuka: RLM 70/71/65. (Illustration by Vincenzo Auletta/ Historical Notes by Stelios Demiras)

German anti-tank aircraft Junkers Ju87G-1 Stuka "Gustav the tank killer" of *Schlachtgeschwader St.G2*, Eastern Front, Battle of Kursk, 1943. This was the personal plane of the famous *Oberleutnant* Hans-Ulrich Rudel. By the end of the war, he had scored an incredible number of kills during more than 2,500 war missions. The Ju 87 Stuka (which is an acronym for *Sturmkampfflugzeug* = dive bomber) first flew in 1935, and went into production in 1937. During the Spanish Civil War it proved itself an excellent weapon for high-value targets, bombing with pinpoint accuracy and justifying the designer's concept. It was in effect meant to be employed as aerial artillery. During WWII, however, its slow speed did not allow it to operate over heavily protected areas or when the *Luftwaffe* could not achieve air superiority and it was soon relegated to other roles, coming into its own as a tank killer in its 'G' version, or *Kanonenvogel*. The Junkers Ju 87G-1 was a modified D version, equipped with two 37mm *Bordkanone* cannon in large pods under the wings, which also included the specially developed tungsten carbide ammunition. Flying the Ju 87G-1, Germany's most celebrated and decorated pilot, Hans-Ulrich Rudel, was credited with a battleship (the Marat), two cruisers, 519 Soviet tanks, 800 other vehicles, and 150 artillery pieces, in addition to having shot down nine aircraft. His famous technique was to attack enemy tanks (usually T-34s) from the rear, where his accurate shooting had better chances of 'brewing' them up. This technique was only possible when the *Luftwaffe* could protect the vulnerable Stukas, otherwise the Ju 87s could become easy kills for the Soviet fighters. The *Stukagruppen* were used in large numbers for the last time during Operation "Zitadelle." The drawing depicts Rudel's personal plane painted in RLM 70/71/65. (Illustration by Vincenzo Auletta / Historical Notes by Stelios Demiras)

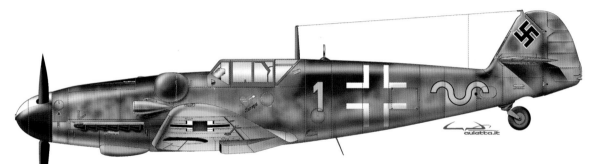

German fighter Messerschmitt Bf 109G-6 of 9/JG52 flown by Lt. Erich Hartmann, Kursk, Russia July 1943. On the first day of the German attack on the Kursk salient, on 5 July 1943, Erich Hartmann flew four missions, and returned from each with a victory. In the next two days, he bagged seven more in four different engagements. On the last day of July, Hartmann's victory tally had reached 41. This plane wears RLM 76 *Lightblau* (Light Gray) overall with upper surface in RLM 74 *Graugrün* (Dark Gray) and RLM 75 *Grauviolett* (Gray Violet). (Illustration by Vincenzo Auletta / Historical Notes by Stelios Demiras)

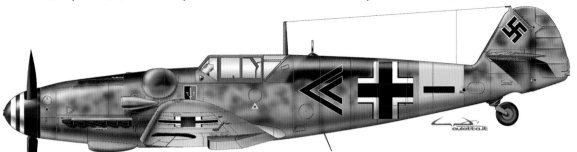

German Messerschmitt Bf 109G-6 fighter flown by *Oberleutnant* Günther Rall of JG 52. Before being promoted to *Hauptmann*, Rall took part in the Battle of Kursk in 1943. During the battle he came close to having a mid-air collision with a Lagg-5 in this plane. This plane sports the typical camouflage pattern of the period: RLM 74/ 75/76. The Bf 109 was the mainstay of the *Luftwaffe* during WW2 and was built in greater numbers than any other fighter before or since. Willy Messerschmitt's original design was revolutionary enough at the time. He designed the smallest possible plane around the most powerful engine then available. No fewer than 35,000 Bf 109s of all versions were produced. Standard armament or the Bf 109G-6 included two MG 131 13mm machineguns in the nose sbove the engine, a 30mm MK 108 cannon firing through the propeller hub and two MG 151 20mm cannon in gondolas under the wings. During the Kursk fighting, the Bf 109G-6s, and the Fw 190A-5s, equipped a number of *Jagdgeschwadern* including: JG 3, JG 51, JG 52 and JG 54. (Illustration by Vincenzo Auletta / Historical Notes by Stelios Demiras)

The Germans launched their final attack from the north in torrential rain on 10 July, with the Ol'khovatka heights as the objective. The 300 armored vehicles of the 2nd and the 3rd Panzer Divisions launched their attack supported by an impressive artillery barrage on the ground and Ju 87s and Heinkel He 111s in the air. They found themselves under constant ground and air assault, however. Eventually, the attack was broken off in the evening, because Model had sustained significant casualties and loss of matériel in his attempt to capture an area no more than 15km wide. The Germans faced fewer difficulties in the south and managed to reach the northernmost point of their advance on 11 July. By this time, the *Luftwaffe* had begun to show signs of battle fatigue and the number of its daily sorties dropped to three digits.

On 12 July, the fighters engaged in a lethal game over the battlefield where the great tank battle of Prokhorovka was taking place. The *Luftwaffe* was first to appear with raids that began at 08.30, giving an

MAJOR GERMAN AIR UNITS	
1. FLIEGERDIVISION (Luftflotte 6)	**LUFTFLOTTE 4**
JG 51 (three groups)	JG 3 (two groups)
JG 54 (one group)	JG 52 (two groups)
KG 3	KG 27
KG 4 (two groups)	KG 51
KG 51 (two groups)	KG 55
KG 53 (two groups)	Sch.G. 1
St.G 1	St.G. 2

German abbreviations-glossary:
Fliegerdivision: air division
JG (Jagdgeschwader): fighter wing
LG (Lehrgeschwader): operational training wing
Luftflotte: air fleet
Sch.G. (Schlachtgeschwader): close support wing
St.G (Sturzkampfgeschwader): dive bomber wing
ZG (Zerstörergeschwader): heavy fighter (twin-engine) aircraft wing
KG: bomber wing

MAJOR SOVIET AIR UNITS	
16. va	**2. va**
1. gv.iad	208. nbad
2. gv.shad	291. szad
283. iad	1. shak
286. iad	1. bak
299. shad	4. iak
3. bak	5. iak
6. sak	6. iak
271. nbad	

Soviet abbreviations-glossary:

bak: bomber air corps
gv.shad: Guards assault division
iak: fighter air corps
sak: mixed air corps
shad: assault division
va: air army

gv.iad: Guards fighter division
iad: fighter division
nbad: night bomber division
shak: assault air corps
szad: assault division

indication of what was to follow. The close support aircraft buzzed over the tanks and infantry like bees around honey. The Soviets succeeded in checking the Germans through this mêlée of tank and aerial combat. One pilot recalls, "the sky was full of planes flying very close to each other. I exchanged glances with an enemy pilot."

The following day, Hitler called off Operation "Zitadelle" after the great Soviet counterattack in the Oryol area and the Allied landings on Sicily on 10 July. The German command needed units engaged in the Battle of Kursk to confront the new dangers. On 19 July, Soviet tanks cut railway communications between Oryol and Bryansk and threatened the 9th Army's main supply route. Most of the close support units were moved to the north to face the new threat. They operated especially effectively, as can be concluded from an excerpt from a 9th Army report to *Luftwaffe* headquarters: "The *Luftwaffe* managed, without any ground support, to check and destroy a tank brigade for the first time in the history of the war."

ATTACK AIRCRAFT TECHNICAL CHARACTERISTICS			
	Ju 87G-1	Hs 129B-2/R-2	Il-2M3
Span (m)	13.8	14.2	14.6
Length (m)	11	9.75	11.65
Height (m)	3.77	3.25	3.40
Wing area (m²)	31.90	29	38.5
Weight empty (kg)	3,900 - 4,400	3,810	3,250
Weight Maximum (kg)	6,600	5,250	6,060
Maximum speed (km/h)	314	407	414
Range (km)	320 – 448	688	600
Engines	1x1,420hp Jumo 211J-1	2x700hp Gnome-Rhône 14M	1x1,780hp AM-38
Armament	2x37mm 2x7.92mm	2x7.92mm 2x20mm 1x30mm	2x7.62mm 1x12.7mm 2x23mm

Opposing Aircraft

The *Luftwaffe* possessed the Fw 190F, Hs 129, and the Ju 87G-1 as close support aircraft. In addition, a large number of Ju 87Ds were available. The D series, powered by the Jumo 211J-1 engine, could carry up to 1,800kg of bombs or a variety of machine-gun pods and fragmentation bombs.

The Soviets' most effective close support aircraft was the Il'yushin Il-2 Shturmovik. During 1943, one in three aircraft coming off the production line was of this type and the monthly output is estimated to have reached around 1,000 aircraft. The Il-2M3 variant had a crew of two and was powerful armed with two 23mm cannons and two 7.62mm machine-guns firing forward and a 12.7mm machine-gun in the rear cockpit. It could also carry 100kg bombs or 82mm rockets. A commonly carried weapon was the PTAB cluster bomb with forty-eight 2.5kg anti-tank bomblets in each. During the Battle of Kursk, it had a casualty rate of almost 3 percent in relation to the total number of sorties flown, while aircraft damaged reached 50 percent. Some Il-2M3s were equipped with a 37mm cannon, which yielded very good

results when used against its intended target – German armor.

In addition, the Soviet Air Force flew the Petlyakov Pe-2 "Peshka" for dive-bombing and against lines of communication. Used effectively during the Battle of Kursk, the Pe-2 carried a crew of three, was armed with four 7.62mm machine-guns and could carry up to 1,000kg of bombs. The first production aircraft were powered by two 1,100hp Klimov M-105P engines but, by 1943, these had been replaced by the more powerful 1,260hp M-105PF.

The Il'yushin Il-4 (DB-3), powered by two 1,100hp M88B engines, was used for long-range missions. It could carry a 2,700kg bomb load and was armed with two 7.62mm and one 12.7mm machine-guns.

The *Luftwaffe*, on the opposing side, fielded the Junkers Ju 88A-4 and the Heinkel He 111 H-6/11/16 of the

A Henschel 129B-2/R2 of 2 Squadron/ *Schlachtgeschwader* **1 before its mission. The 30mm MK 101 cannon, without its characteristic cover, is visible under the fuselage. The Hs 129s were specialized anti-tank aircraft but no more than 60 operated on the Eastern Front.**

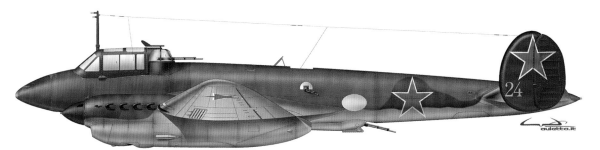

Soviet (dive) bomber Petlyakov Pe-2 *Peshka*, s/n 24 of the 40th BAP. This airplane was photographed with another four during a mission against German troops during the battle of Kursk, Russian Front, 1943. The Pe-2 was undoubtedly the best dive bomber of the Soviet air forces during WW2, being fast and very agile, since it had originally been designed as a heavy escort fighter. Vladimir Petlyakov designed it from prison having been accused by the lunatic Soviet leader of being a 'saboteur' in 1937. The plane was so successful that Stalin freed Petlyakov and allowed him to use his name on the type. It was powered by two Klimov VK-105 RF rated at 1,200hp each, armed with one or two Berezin HMGs and two MGs and could carry a useful bomb load of 1,000kg. Air superiority at Kursk was of major importance for both combattants and required an enormous amount of air power to be committed. The Pe-2 was mainly used against soft targets and interdiction roles and caused much consternation to rear area units of the 9th German Army. The aircraft depicted sports a Light Green, Earth Brown, Gray and Dark Green camouflage scheme on the top surfaces and Underside Blue Grey beneath. (Illustration by Vincenzo Auletta/Historical Notes by Stelios Demiras)

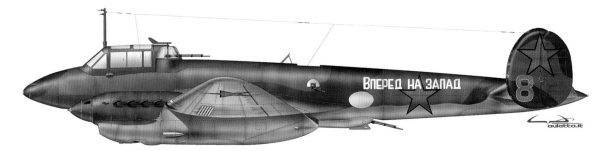

Soviet (dive) bomber Petlyakov Pe-2 *Peshka* Serial No. 8 *Vperyod na Zapad* during the battle of Kursk. It was one of the planes of the 115 series, painted in a two-tone green camouflage. The specific aircraft is in Light green and Dark Green upper surfaces and Dark Gray under. (Illustration by Vincenzo Auletta / Historical Notes by Stelios Demiras)

KG 3/4/27/53 and 55 Bomber Wings. The Ju 88A-4 was the foremost bomber variant of the family and could carry a bomb load up to 2,500kg on four wing racks with a further 500kg in the bomb bay. Its defensive armament included up to eight 7.92mm machine-guns. The He 111H series was powered by the Jumo 211F-2, and could carry a bomb load of eight 250kg bombs or one 2,000kg bomb and one of 500kg on external racks. They had a very effective defensive armament of one 20mm cannon, a 13mm machine-gun, and up to seven 7.92 mm machine-guns.

The Messerschmitt Bf 109G-6 and the Focke-Wulf Fw 190A were the foremost German fighters. The Bf 109G-6 was the most numerous

variant of the marque and was developed with the idea of fitting it with different field conversions (weapons kits), depending on the required operational tasks. The first production aircraft had a 20mm MG 151/20 20mm cannon, firing through the propeller hub, and two 13mm MG 131s. The more powerful 30mm MK108 gradually replaced the MG 151/20 from mid-1943. This version could carry a 300-liter drop tank or a 250kg bomb on the central bomb rack. It could also be armed with two 20mm cannons in underwing gun pods.

The Fw 190A-4/A-5 was powered by a 1,700hp BMW 801D engine and armed with four 20mm cannons and two 7.92mm machine-guns. The

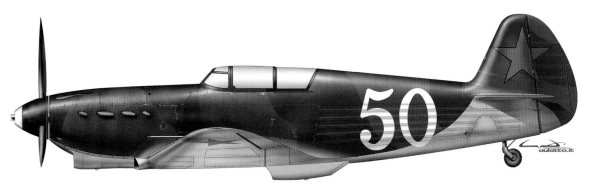

Soviet fighter Yakovlev Yak-1 s/n 50 of the 18th GvIAP, flown in the Kursk sector by GvIAP Lt.. Colonel Anatoly Yemel'yanovich Golubov, Spring 1943. The Yak-1 was the first of a series of relatively nimble fighters of rather basic 'no-frills' design and construction. It was nevertheless easy to build and easier to maintain and was an adequate performer at low level, severely handicapped higher up. It was relatively lightly armed with a single 20mm cannon and two 7.62mm MGs. The Yak family of fighters was numerically the most significant in the Soviet WW2 arsenal with 8,721 Yak-1s built. Following the Kursk campaign, the Red Air Force began to gain the upper hand   strategically, which grew to crushing proportions by the end of the conflict. (Illustration by Vincenzo Auletta/Historical Notes by Stelios Demiras)

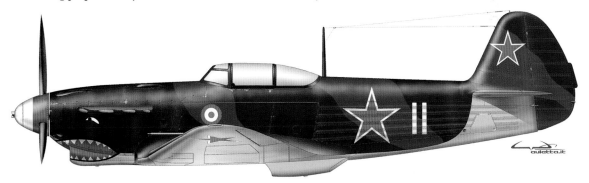

Soviet fighter Yakovlev Yak-1b s/n 11 of the Groupe de Chasse *Normandie* and flown by pilot Albert Durand during the spring of 1943. Based at Oryol, the French piloted *Normandie* – Niemen flew Yaks into battles over Kursk. This plane wears a three-color camouflage with the upper surfaces in Dark Olive Green A24M and Black AMT 6 over Light Blue Gray AMT-7 for under surfaces. This French Groupe de Chasse (originally a Squadron – until Autumn 1943) composed of Free French volunteers made a significant effort to regaining some of the prestige the French Air Force had lost in 1940. By the end of its involvement, some 95 Frenchmen had flown in Soviet fighters and 42 had lost their lives in combat. They had flown a total of 5,240 sorties, fought in 869 engagements and claimed 273 kills. In August 1944, by order of Stalin himself, the Groupe was officially renamed *Normandie - Niemen*, in recognition of the French pilots' contribution to the Soviet Army's success in crossing the Niemen river. (Illustration by Vincenzo Auletta/Historical Notes by Stelios Demiras)

Fw190F series were A-series fighter-bombers with additional armor plating to protect the engine and cockpit areas. It could carry a 500kg bomb on its central bomb rack, but the usual load was one 250kg and four 50kg bombs. Its major characteristics were its performance and high load capacity, but the aircraft was always in short supply.

The Soviet Air Force also lined up a series of efficient aircraft, having learned the hard lessons it had been taught by the Germans during previous operations. The Yak fighter family was designed by the Yakovlev Design Bureau, including the Yak-1M, Yak-7, Yak-9 and Yak-3. The Yak-1M Moskit, a great improvement over the Yak-1, was fitted with a new canopy, retractable landing gear, and other modifications. It had the M-105PF engine and was armed with a 20mm cannon and a 12.7mm machine gun. The Yak-9 became operational on November 1942, and retained the

FIGHTER AIRCRAFT TECHNICAL CHARACTERISTICS

	Bf 109G-6	Fw 190A-3	La-5FN	Yak-9D
Span (m)	9.92	10.51	9.8	9.74
Length (m)	9.03	8.8	8.67	8.55
Height (m)	2.50	3.9	2.54	3
Wing area (m²)	16.10	18.30	17.59	17.15
Weight empty (kg)	2,673	3,225	2,678	2,770
Weight Maximum (kg)	3,400	3,977	3,322	3,080
Maximum speed (km/h)	621	673	620	602
Range (km)	998	1,035	580	1,400
Engine	1x1,475hp DB605AM	1x1,700hp BMW 801D-2	1x1,470hp ASh-82FN	1x1,360hp M-105PF-3
Armament	2x13mm 1x20mm	4x20mm 4x7.92mm	2x20mm	1x20mm 1-2x12.7mm
Rate of climb (m/min)	1,020	1,050	1,064	834

BOMBER AIRCRAFT TECHNICAL CHARACTERISTICS

	He 111H-16	Ju 88A-4	Il-4	Pe-2
Span (m)	22.6	20.08	21.44	17.2
Length (m)	16.40	14.36	14.76	12.6
Height (m)	4	4.85	4.2	3.5
Wing area (m²)	86.50	54.5	66.70	40.5
Weight empty (kg)	8,680	8,000	5,800	5,870
Weight Maximum (kg)	14,000	14,000	9,470	8,520
Maximum speed (km/h)	405	433	335	540
Range (km)	2,060	1,790	2,600	1,200
Engines	2x1,340hp Jumo 211F-2	2x1,340hp Jumo 211J	2x1,100hp M-88B	2x1,100hp M-105P
Defensive armament	1x20mm 1x13mm Up to 7x7.92mm	Up to 8x7.92 mm	2x7.62mm 1x12.7mm	4x7.62mm
Bomb load (kg)	2,500	3,000	2,700	1,000

armament of the earlier Yak fighters. The Yak-9D entered service in May 1943, with additional fuel tanks on the wings and an up-rated 1,360hp M-105PF-3 engine.

A small number of Yak-3s and La-5FNs, from the Lavochkin Design Bureau, were tested during the Battle of Kursk. The Yak-3 was the smallest and most maneuverable aircraft of its category and weighed less than 2,600kg. With the 1,300hp M-105PF-2 engine, it had a maximum speed of 655km/h at a height of 3,100m. Its armament consisted of one 20mm cannon, firing through the propeller hub, and two 12.7mm machine-guns. The first La-5FN was an improved version of the La-5 with ASh-82FN engines, rated at 1,850hp at take off, and armed with two 20mm cannons.

They were among the most dangerous opponents faced by the *Luftwaffe* during the summer and fall of 1943. The first production aircraft were on operational trials with the 32nd Guards Fighter Regiment, one of the best units at the front. Its pilots flew 25 missions during the Battle of Kursk and shot down 33 German aircraft (21 Fw 190As among them,) for the loss of just six La-5FNs. One of its pilots, Hero of the Soviet Union Captain Vladimir Ivanovich Garanin, commented that "dogfights took place at heights up to 4,000m and our aircraft were superior to the Bf 109 and the Fw 190, both in speed and maneuverability."

A little known pilot, 23-year-old Ivan Nikitovich Kozhedub, scored his first kill – a Ju 87 – on 6 July during

The Petlyakov Pe-2, similar to the Mosquito, proved especially effective at both high level and as a dive bomber.

the Battle of Kursk. He shot down another Stuka the following day and two Bf 109s on 8 July. By war's end, Kozhedub had scored a total of 62 kills and become one of the leading Allied aces. His recollections from his first victory and the battle are indicative of the prevailing conditions, "Our orders were to attack a formation of Ju 87 Stuka bombers. I chose my victim and flew close to him. It was all done in fractions of a second and, only later could I recall the details while on the ground. Pilots who knew their plane very well and acted instinctively were the ones who could shoot down an enemy aircraft. Our missions during the Battle of Kursk included bomber escort, flying against enemy fighters, and eliminating anti-aircraft batteries. The battle was a turning point for our operational methods. During the first phase of the battle, our aviators flew 70,219 sorties, destroyed 1,500 aircraft against 1,000 losses on our side. Seventy-six percent of the missions were tactical, 18 percent long-range missions, with the remainder air defense. Our aviators flew 90,000 sorties during the counterattack, 50 percent of which were close support and 31 percent air

superiority sorties. The enemy had lost about 2,200 aircraft up to that time." While the total of German losses claimed by Kozhedub are probably more than the total number of available *Luftwaffe* aircraft, it is nevertheless a fact that the Battle of Kursk was a milestone in air operations. It is estimated that by 15 July, the *Luftwaffe* had lost 196 aircraft, while Soviet losses were even greater. The 2nd Air Army had lost 153 aircraft by 10 July. Following the Battle of Kursk, German forces were in a continuous retreat that did not stop until the fall of Berlin in 1945.

A Bf 109G-6 of *Jagdgeschwader* (Fighter Wing) JG 3 "Udet" with a 250kg bomb under the fuselage. The need to support the attack was especially pressing and even fighters were used for close support missions.

The PzKpfw V Panther
and PzKpfw VI Tiger at Kursk

Among the hundreds of tanks that advanced towards Soviet lines in the area of Kursk on 5 July 1943 were two of Germany's latest models. The Tiger had already been in production for a year and had proved its worth on the Eastern Front. The Panther, straight off the production line, had not yet been cured of its "teething troubles." Although they accounted for only a small proportion of the total number of tanks engaged, the Panthers and Tigers made a significant contribution on the fronts where they operated. In the end, however, they could not change the final outcome of the battle.

On 3 and 4 May 1943, the German Führer Adolf Hitler; the German High Command; Günther von Kluge, the Commander of the Army Group "Center"; Erich von Manstein, the Commander of Army Group "North"; Walter Model, the Commander of the 9th Army; Albert Speer, the Minister of Armaments; and Heinz Guderian, the Inspector-General of Panzer troops, all gathered in Munich for a conference of extraordinary significance. Two lines of argument were elaborated. The Chief of the General Staff, General Kurt Zeitzler, asked for an attack to be undertaken on the Eastern Front. He believed that the heavy PzKpfw VI Tiger tank and the new PzKpfw V Panther tank would enable Germany to regain the initiative in military operations. Guderian, however, believed that an

A German Panther Ausf D medium tank, Kursk, 1943. The Panther was the German answer to the introduction of the Soviet T-34 and the German design took into consideration the advantages of the sloped armor of the Soviet tank. The too-hasty mass production of the Panther initially created many problems because Germany's industrial capacity was limited. The first operational use of the Panthers was at Kursk and the majority of the tanks were soon put out of action, due mostly to mechanical breakdowns rather than enemy action. The Panthers proved to be a near-perfect combination of armor, speed, and firepower after the initial problems had been overcome. Total production was 5,976 units. It weighed 43 tons, had a maximum armor thickness of 100mm (on the machine-gun mantlet) and a top speed of 45km/h. It was armed with the Rheinmetall 7.5cm KwK 42 L/70 gun and two 7.92mm MG 34 machine guns. This tank of an unknown unit is finished in a two-color scheme with Sand Yellow as the basic color and irregular stripes in Olive Green or Dark Green. (Illustration by Dimitris Hadoulas/ Historical Note by Stelios Demiras)

GERMAN *KANONIER* (ARTILLERYMAN), KURSK 1943
He wears the standard-issue field gray service dress (M40 tunic and trousers) and M1939 Jackboots (marching boots) with M42 helmet. He sports a Winter Campaign Medal 1941-1942 "Frozen Meat." Note the *Waffenfarbe* (Arm of Service color) red for artillery. This *Kanonier* holds a Flak 8.8cm shell and is wearing the minimum of equipment. M1939 leather infantry support straps and leather belt. (Illustration by Johnny Shumate / Historical Notes-Comments by Stelios Demiras)

attack would result in so many tank losses that it would not be possible to replace them during 1943. In addition, the new Panther tanks had not overcome the initial mechanical problems inherent in all new weapon systems and correcting them in a reasonable time frame did not seem possible. Von Kluge agreed with Zeitzler while Speer sided with Guderian. Hitler, like Manstein, remained skeptical and no final decision was taken. Hitler pondered over the matter for a considerable time before, finally, taking the decision to launch Operation "Zitadelle" (Citadel), the elimination of the Kursk salient. The date set for the launch of the attack was 5 July 1943.

The PzKpfw VI Ausf E Tiger

Germany's most famous tank, the Tiger, was born in 1937, when the Henschel company was ordered to design and build a 30-33-ton tank as a possible successor to the PzKpfw IV. Characteristic of the new vehicle, dubbed the DW I (*Durchbruchwagen*, Breakthrough Tank) were its overlapping, interleaved road wheels.

Further specifications were laid down during the following years with the main competitors being Henschel and Porsche. Many different designs and prototypes had been planned, among them a 65-ton tank, an improved DW II model with a short 7.5cm gun and a 36-ton tank with a maximum speed of at least 40km/h, but in May 1941, all these experiments halted. The final order laid down plans for a 45-ton tank that would be armed with a version of the successful 8.8cm anti-aircraft gun.

Henschel and Porsche incorporated the best elements of their experimental models into the new design, and two prototypes, dubbed the VK4501(H) and VK4501(P), respectively, for the two companies, were demonstrated to Hitler on his birthday on 20 April 1942. The Henschel design was preferred and accepted. The new tank was given the designation PzKpfw VI Tiger Ausf E, or Tiger I. Over the following two years (August 1942-August 1944) 1,350 were built (of an initial order of 1,376 tanks). In addition, 90 Tigers were ordered to be built by Porsche, partly as a precaution against delays in Henschel's production.

The Tiger I was the first German tank in production to have triple overlapping steel road wheels with solid rubber tires and correspondingly positioned suspension. This system was adopted for optimum weight distribution. There were eight independently-sprung torsion-bar axles on each side, giving an extremely soft and stable ride for a tank of this weight and size. Two types of track were used; one, 725mm in width, was fitted for combat conditions, and the other, of 520mm (without the outer wheels), for travel and transportation.

The interleaved wheels system also had its disadvantages. The wheels were liable to become packed with mud and snow, and if they were not kept clear, they would also freeze and jam. The Soviets discovered this weakness and took advantage of it by timing their attacks for dawn, when the vehicles were more likely to have become immobilised during the night's frost.

The Tiger's hull, typical of a German tank, consisted of four compartments: the forward two housed the driver and hull gunner/radio-operator, the central was the fighting compartment, and the engine compartment was placed at the rear. The gearbox separated the two

A Panther Ausf D with side skirts (*Schürzen*). The driver sits behind the left hatch with the radio operator/machine gunner on the right. The machine gunner had a hatch that opened vertically on the first Ausf D models and he fired his MG 34 machine gun through it.

forward compartments. The driver sat on the left and steered the vehicle by means of a wheel which acted hydraulically on the differential steering unit. The radio-operator was seated on the right and he also manned the MG 34 machine-gun.

In order to simplify assembly and allow the use of solid, heavy armor plate, the tank was manufactured with the maximum possible use of large flat sections. An innovative feature was the welding of the hull and superstructure (where previous tanks had bolted joints). The top, forward hull plate covered the full width of the vehicle, permitting a large enough turret ring to be fitted to accommodate the 8.8cm gun.

The fighting compartment had its own base, suspended from the turret by three steel tubes. The breech mechanism divided the area into two. Like the hull, the turret was a simple structure with its sides and rear formed from a single 82mm-thick plate curved in a horseshoe fashion with the front being joined by two 100mm-thick rectangular bars. The commander's cupola had five vision slits and was of a plain, cylindrical appearance.

The 8.8cm KwK 36 gun had ballistic characteristics similar to those of the famed anti-aircraft gun of the same caliber from which it derived. The principal modifications were the addition of a muzzle brake (to absorb the recoil) and electric firing. A co-axial MG 34 was fired by mechanical linkage from a foot pedal operated by the gunner. Elevation and hand traverse were controlled by hand wheels and a hydraulic power traverse was controlled by a rocking footplate operated by the gunner.

The Tiger was recognized as the most advanced tank in service due to its powerful gun and armor. It was expensive to build, however, and difficult to adapt to a series production line.

The PzKpfw V Ausf D Panther

"Numerous Russian T-34s went into action and inflicted heavy losses on the German tanks at Mtsensk in 1941... I wrote a detailed report on the situation, which, for us, was a novel situation, and sent it to the Army Group ... . In this report, I described

PANTHER PANZER BATTALION ORGANIZATION (KURSK 1943)	
Panzer Battalion Command	Signals Platoon (3xBefehlswagen Panther SdKfz 267/268)
	Reconnaissance Platoon (5xPanther)
	Service Platoon (2xBergepanther)
Panzer Company (x 4)	Company Command (2xPanther)
	Panzer Platoon (5xPanther)
	Panzer Platoon (5xPanther)
	Panzer Platoon (5xPanther)
	Panzer Platoon (5xPanther)
Theoretical strength: 93 Panthers + 3 Command Panthers	

TIGER PANZER BATTALION ORGANIZATION (KURSK 1943)		
Panzer Battalion Command	3 Tiger	
Headquarters Company	Signals Platoon (3 Befehlspanzer)	
	Light Panzer Platoon (10xPz III/IV)	
	Light Platoon (5xPz II)	
	Reconnaissance and Engineer Platoon	Reconnaissance Section (x4)
		Engineer Section (x3)
	Anti-aircraft Platoon	Anti-aircraft Section (x3)
Panzer Company (x 4)	Company Command (2xTiger)	
	Panzer Platoon (4xTiger)	
	Panzer Platoon (4xTiger)	
	Panzer Platoon (4xTiger)	
Theoretical strength: 59 Tiger, 10 Panzer III/IV, 5 Panzer II		

in plain terms the marked superiority of the T-34 over our PzKpfw IV and drew the relevant conclusion that this must affect our future tank production. I concluded by urging a commission be sent immediately to my sector of the front." The above was written by the then 2nd Panzer Group (*Panzergruppe*) Commander, General Heinz Guderian, in whose sector the T-34 was first encountered in large numbers during November 1941.

On the 25 November 1941, having received the report of the commission requested by Guderian, the Army Weapons Agency (*Heereswaffenamt*) contracted the Daimler-Benz and Maschinenfabrik Augsburg Nürnberg (MAN) firms to produce designs for a new medium tank, in the 30-35-ton class, to be ready by the following spring. The tank would have 60mm frontal armor, a 75mm gun and sloped armor on the front and sides, like the T-34. The two designs were submitted in April. The Daimler-Benz proposal was an almost direct copy of the Soviet tank with the addition of a few refinements. The turret was mounted well forward and included the driver's seat. Paired steel bogies (without rubber tires) were suspended by leaf springs.

Hitler was impressed with the Daimler-Benz proposal, although he suggested that the 75mm gun be changed from the proposed L/48 model to the longer L/70. However, the Army Weapons Agency preferred the MAN design, as some of the T-34's mechanical features were impractical for the German manufacturers to copy.

The MAN design called for a higher, wider hull, with a large turret placed well back. Torsion bar suspension was used with interleaved road wheels, while a petrol engine was proposed, with the drive through the front sprockets. The internal layout followed conventional German practice, with stations for the driver and hull gunner/radio-operator in the forward compartment.

Militarily, it was necessary to start mass production by December 1942, but Daimler-Benz was unable to meet the deadline. The MAN design was presented to Hitler and was accepted in May 1942. At the same time, the specifications for the frontal armor were restated, increasing its thickness to 80mm, the change increasing the weight to 44 tons. However, the wheels and suspension system planned for the original vehicle had already been completed, with the subcontractors working from the original plans. As a result, the components designed for the original vehicle were subjected to additional strain, leading to problems of unreliability.

The first MAN prototype was completed in September 1942 and tested at its Nuremberg factory. The second was officially tested at the Army Weapons Agency's test range in Kummersdorf. The Panthers, which began leaving the MAN factory in November 1942, were designated PzKpfw V Panther Ausf A, and were "pre-production" models with 60mm frontal armor thickness. The "final" models appeared in January 1943. The first production type was the Ausf D, with characteristics that made

it easily recognizable: the small commander's cupola with six vision slits, the round hatch on the left side of the turret, the double hole in the gun mantlet for the aiming device, the observation hatch and the slit on the hull, shaped like a letter-box, that was covered by a jointed armored plate in the machine-gun port and the smoke dischargers on the turret sides. The Panther's turret housed its five-member crew and was arranged in the same way as all German-built tanks.

The 80mm glacis plate was sloped at 33 degrees to the horizontal, an angle specifically designed to deflect shells striking the glacis upwards and clear of the mantlet. The 7.5cm KwK 42 L/70 gun was developed by Rheinmetall and was fitted with a muzzle baffle that absorbed 70 percent of the recoil when firing.

The first deliveries began in February 1943, but then halted in April with all Panthers (about 300) being recalled to the factory for some major modifications demanded by the increase in weight. In May 1943, the 51st and 52nd Tank Battalions were equipped with the first Panther Ausf Ds.

A Tiger tank from 3./5. Panzer Abteilung 503. The crews have a break after stopping their Tigers on the side of the track.

On each side, the Panther had a double torsion-bar suspension for the four inner and outer road wheels, an idler wheel with an adjusting shaft for track tensioning, two shock absorbers and a drive sprocket. The first, third, fifth, and seventh wheels from the front were double, while the intervening axles carried spaced wheels overlapping the others on the inside and outside. The interleaved running gear gave the Panther equal ground pressure and the vertical movement of the road wheels was small, even while traversing rugged terrain. The design also had a number of disadvantages, such as the difficulty of replacing components after damage (e.g. by a mine) and the accumulation of mud, earth, and ice. In addition, one damaged wheel often required the removal of several road wheels.

In the interval between the Munich conference and the beginning of Operation "Zitadelle," Guderian worked hard to solve the Panther's technical problems quickly, while also attempting to have the attack postponed. On 25 May, he visited the Nibelungen factory in Linz, that was producing the new tanks, and on 1 June, he visited Grafenwöhr where he inspected the 51st and 52nd Tank Battalions (*Panzer Abteilung*), the first units to be equipped with the Panther Ausf D. He reported, on 15 June, that the suspension and steering systems had to be improved and that the aiming device was unsatisfactory. During his talk with Hitler on 16 June, Guderian outlined the problems encountered with the new tank. A second visit to Grafenwöhr on 18 June revealed that the tank commanders and their crews were in desperate need of proper training on the type, while quite a few of them were without any combat experience.

Organization

The mission of the heavy tanks was to support the panzer divisions, serving as the "hammer" at the point where resistance was toughest, or as a "fort" where the enemy's attack was strongest. For this reason, the Tigers were assigned to independent heavy tank battalions (*schwere Panzer Abteilung – sPzAbt*) under the command of a corps or a higher formation. The panzer divisions that were going to engage in operations would receive a number of Tigers so they could spearhead the attack. Because of their limited maneuverability on the one hand, and their low speed on the other, however, the deployment of lighter tanks in support platoons was deemed necessary, with the PzKpfw IIIs and IVs usually tasked with this. The theoretical strength of each heavy tank battalion was 59 tanks: three tanks assigned to the battalion headquarters, four companies with two command tanks and three platoons of four tanks each. In reality, no battalion possessed a fourth company, while the ones with three were considered fortunate.

Later, it was decided to have the Tigers become organic to the panzer divisions. Guderian's intention was to include one heavy tank battalion to the table of organization of each panzer division, but their scarcity did not allow for their assignment to some favored Army and *Waffen-SS* divisions. The first Tigers were assigned to the 1st SS Panzer Grenadier Division *Leibstandarte Adolf Hitler* (1.SS-Panzergrenadier Division *Leibstandarte Adolf Hitler* or 1.SS-PzGrenDiv 'LSSAH') and to the 2nd SS Panzer Grenadier Division *Das Reich* in company-strength and organic to their panzer regiments. By the start of the Battle of Kursk, the 3rd SS Panzer

Grenadier Division *Totenkopf,* had also been equipped with a Tiger company.

A panzer regiment of 1943 consisted of eight companies in two battalions. The Panthers, as the PzKpfw IVs replacements-to-be, would theoretically equip one battalion of each regiment. Their battalion strength was to be 51 tanks in the Army tank battalions and 62 tanks in the SS tank battalions. Production was unable to meet demand, however, and the few Panthers at the Battle of Kursk (assigned to two independent tank battalions) operationally used the Tiger tactics to locally reinforce a higher formation's firepower. In the past it was reported that the 1st Tank Battalion of the *Grossdeutschland* Tank Regiment was equipped with 80 Panthers and that a small number of Panthers had been assigned to the three divisions. Information now available indicates that this report was erroneous.

Instructions drawn from pamphlets (*Merkblatt*) 47a/29 and 47a/30 issued in May 1943 were used by the heavy tanks during attacks by panzer units. The typical armor wedge (*Panzerkeil*) attack formation was used during the battles to eliminate the Kursk salient. The tanks would form a wedge-shaped formation with the commander's tank at the base so he could control and coordinate the remainder of the formation.

Heavy Tanks at Kursk

The Tiger E had first appeared on the Leningrad front in 1942, and its presence was deeply felt on the southern front during the February 1943 battles. At Kursk, there were 148 Tigers (various sources state numbers between 146 and 181) or 57 percent of all available Tigers, 15 of which were command tanks (*Befehlpanzer*).

The Army's 503rd Heavy Tank Battalion, assigned to Army Detachment Kempf, was equipped with 48 Tigers. The three SS mechanized divisions that formed II SS Panzer Corps each had one Tiger company. A 13th Company had been added to the 'LSSAH' Tank Regiment, which consisted of three battalions. The *Das Reich* and *Totenkopf* Tank Regiments, each of which consisted of

German Tiger tank, flanked by an SdKfz 251 armored personnel carrier column. Both belong to the élite German Division *Grossdeutschland* that was equipped with 15 Tiger tanks during the Battle of Kursk.

TIGER TECHNICAL SPECIFICATIONS
PzKpfw VI (Tiger) Ausf E (SdKfz 181)

	Front	Side	Rear	Top / Bottom
Crew	5			
Weight	57t			
Length	8.45m			
Width	3.7m			
Height	2.93m			
Armor	Front	Side	Rear	Top / Bottom
Hull (upper)	100mm / 10°	80mm / 0°		25mm / 90mm
Hull (lower)	100mm / 24°	60mm / 0°	80mm / 8°	25mm / 90mm
Turret	100mm / 8°	80mm / 0°	80mm / 0°	25mm / 90mm
Gun Mantlet	100 – 110mm / 0°	-	-	-
Engine type	Maybach HL 210 P45 V-12 (600hp at 3,000rpm)			
Engine displacement	21,353cm³			
Maximum speed	38km/h on roads, 20km/h cross-country			
Range	140km			
Radio	FuG5 (bandwidth 27.2Mhz – 33.3Mhz)			
Main armament	8.8cm Kw.K. 36 L/56 (onboard storage capacity 92 rounds)			
Barrel bore & length	56 caliber/4.93 m			
Traverse	360° (hydraulic)			
Elevation	-9° to +10°			
Initial muzzle velocity	773m/sec (Pzgr. 39,) 930m/sec (Pzgr. 40)			
Shell weight	10.2kg (Pzgr. 39,) 7.3kg (Pzgr. 40)			
Secondary armament	One co-axial and one hull-mounted MG 34 7.92mm (4,800 rounds)			
Gun sight	TZF9b x 26'1 or TZF9c x 25'1 (magnification 2.5x)			

NOTE: *Armor is the thickness of the plate and the deflection angle from the vertical*

two battalions, had exchanged their 8th Company tanks for Tigers. An additional heavy tank company was added to the *Grossdeutschland* Tank Regiment of the army panzer grenadier division of the same name that was assigned to the XLVIII Panzer Corps. The three SS divisions had 13, 14, and 15 tanks respectively, the *Grossdeutschland* 14, giving a total of 56 Tigers in the 4th Panzer Army.

By May 1943, 324 Panthers were in service, most of them on the Eastern Front. Each of the 51st and 53rd Tank Battalions was in the process of being equipped with 96 Panther Ausf Ds. With the 911th Assault Gun Battalion, they formed the 10th Panzer Brigade, which was assigned to the 4th Panzer Army. All these units were concentrated at the southern end of the German pincer around the Kursk salient, under Army Group South.

The 9th Army (Army Group Center) was in the north of the salient and was supported by the 505th Heavy Tank Battalion. At the beginning of the battle, this unit had two companies, each with 15 Tigers. A 3rd Company (14 tanks) was added three days after the launch of the attack on Kursk. This battalion formed the 21st Panzer Brigade, which also included the 216th Tank Battalion (equipped with *Brummbar* self-propelled heavy mortars).

The two 505th Heavy Tank Battalion companies operated with the 6th Infantry Division on the 9th Army front during the morning of 5 July 1943. The Tigers moved off three hours after the infantry and, after destroying a defensive outpost equipped with T-34s and anti-tank guns, stormed into the Oka River valley, and onto the exposed flank of

PANTHER TECHNICAL SPECIFICATIONS			
PzKpfw V (Panther) Ausf D (SdKfz 171)			
Crew	5		
Weight	43t		
Length	8.86m		
Width	3.4m		
Height	2.95m		
Armor	Front	Side	Rear	Top / Bottom
Hull (upper)	80mm / 55°	40mm / 40°	-	16mm / 90mm
Hull (lower)	60mm / 55°	40mm / 0°	40mm / 30°	30mm / 90mm
Turret	100mm / 10°	45mm / 25°	45mm / 25°	16mm / 90mm
Gun Mantlet	100mm (round)	-	-	-
Engine type	Maybach HL230 P30 V-12 (650hp at 3,000rpm)		
Engine displacement	23,095cm^3		
Maximum speed	46km/h on roads, 24km/h cross-country		
Range	200km		
Radio	FuG5 (bandwidth 27.2Mhz – 33.3Mhz)		
Main armament	7.5cm Kw.K.42 L/70 (onboard storage capacity 79 rounds)		
Barrel bore & length	70 caliber/5.25m		
Traverse	360° (hydraulic)		
Elevation	-8° to +18°		
Initial muzzle velocity	925m/sec (Pzgr. 39/42,) 1,120m/sec (Pzgr. 40/42)		
Shell weight	6.80kg (Pzgr. 39/42,) 4.75kg (Pzgr. 40/42)		
Secondary armament	One co-axial and one hull-mounted MG 34 7.92mm (5,100 rounds)		
Gun sight	TZF 12X28'1 (magnification 2.5x)		

NOTE: *Armor is the thickness of the plate and the deflection angle from the vertical*

the Soviet 676th Rifle Regiment. Major Bernhard Sauvant's tanks captured the village of Butyrki and were threatening to unhinge the left flank of the Soviet 81st Rifle Division. The 505th Heavy Tank Battalion Tigers were placed under the command of the 2nd Panzer Division during the following day, 6 July, and by taking advantage of their strong armor and firepower, attacked and occupied Soborovka. The remaining Tigers spearheaded the attack on the carefully-planned defenses between the villages Soborovka and Ponyri, but failed to break through. That evening, numerous Tigers from both companies, as well as other German tanks lay smoldering or abandoned within Soviet lines. The attempt by the 3rd Company to penetrate the Soviet defenses at Tyoploye on 7 July was also unsuccessful.

Guderian's worst fears before the start of the battle on the 4th Panzer Army front had come true: the Panthers were not ready for combat. The approach roads from the railheads to the concentration areas were clogged with broken-down tanks immobilized by faulty steering systems or overheated engines that had burst into flames. The Panthers of the 10th Panzer Brigade made their debut with the *Grossdeutschland* Division infantry in the first line. Bad luck continued to dog them, however, and, right after the start, they found themselves in an enemy minefield that had not been cleared. The panzers were immobilized and casualties rose. When they at last were recovered with the help of the engineers, they advanced to support the major part of the *Grossdeutschland* Division. The *Grossdeutschland* heavy tank company

The T-34 Model 1943 was the most numerous variant of the Soviet tank that the Panthers and Tigers encountered in July 1943.

Tigers along with the 10th Panzer Brigade Panthers, in support of the other divisional tanks, broke through the Soviet lines close to Cherkasskoye and, following a fierce battle, found themselves in front of the village.

The appearance of the new tank had caused disquiet in the Soviet lines. A Soviet radio message on 8 July 1943 reported: "Enemy is using a new tank. Silhouette like the T-34. Tank heavily armored, weight estimated between 40 and 50 tons. Armament probably 88mm anti-aircraft gun. We have sustained casualties at ranges beyond 2,000m." The Germans, however, were painfully aware that most Panther casualties during the first day of the battle were due to mechanical problems and not to enemy action and that the available tanks were thus reduced from almost 200 to 40. Notwithstanding the Soviets' surprise and trepidation at the appearance of the new tank, the unfavorable situation did not change for the Panthers. During the following days, mechanical breakdowns put even more tanks put out of action, with many of them being lost for good when the enemy reoccupied lost ground.

On 5 July, the II SS Panzer Corps launched its attack to the north and

managed to penetrate the Soviet lines to a depth of around 20 kilometers by the end of the day. The 42 Tigers of the three mechanized divisions spearheading the tank "wedge" no doubt played a major role in the advance, by allowing it to pass "through" the anti-tank barrage and artillery positions of the 52nd Guards Division. The German tank ace Michael Wittmann was with them, fighting with the 'LSSAH' Tank Regiment's 13th Company, having begun his career in Tigers. During the first day of the battle, Wittmann destroyed two anti-tank guns and a T-34 and also saved the platoon of another tank ace, Helmutt Wendorf, when it got into trouble.

The II SS Panzer Corps continued its advance with the help of the Tigers, causing heavy casualties in the enemy camp. On 8 July, about 40 T-34s of the 3rd Mechanized Corps encountered the *Grossdeutschland* Tiger company. Ten T-34s were destroyed in the ensuing battle and the rest withdrew. The Soviet defense line was forced as much as 20km back south of Oboyan' on the morning of 9 July, with heavy Russian casualties. In the evening, the axis of attack moved to the northeast and the town of Prokhorovka. In contrast with the other fronts, the 48 Tigers of the 503rd Heavy Tank Battalion did not manage to assist Army Detachment Kempf during the launch of the operation. The Tigers were fighting between the multiple Soviet defensive lines until 10 July. The next day, however, they succeeded in breaking through to the last line of the Soviet defenses and began advancing to the north over open ground. They had reached the approaches of Prokhorovka from the south when night fell.

The Battle of Kursk reached its culmination in a mass tank

engagement near Prokhorovka, beginning on 12 July. Hundreds of tanks of the German 4th Panzer Army and the Soviet 5th Guards Tank Army took part in the greatest tank battle in history.

As was typical, the Tigers formed the spearhead of the German attack. The Soviet reaction took the German crews by surprise, however, as the Russians accelerated towards the approaching enemy tanks. It was a well-calculated move. The aim was to lessen the advantage the Tigers possessed due to their heavy 8.8cm gun and its capacity to score accurate hits at long range on the lighter Soviet tanks. The Tigers were stopping to fire at the enemy tanks, but the Soviets were trying to pass them and then aim at their vulnerable points. "Our tanks destroyed the Tigers at close range, where the Germans could not take advantage of their superior armament. We knew their vulnerable points and

our crews shot at their sides. The shells, fired from close range, opened huge holes in the Tigers' armor. Ammunition exploded and the turrets, weighing quite a few tons, were hurled many meters away." In addition, according to official Soviet history, "Close combat deprived the Tigers of the advantage they had due to their heavy gun and armor, resulting in the T-34s' successfully shooting at them from close range."

Individual successes could not win the battle for the Germans. For example, some 'LSSAH' Tigers managed to repulse a Soviet 181st Tank Regiment attack. The engagement with the Soviet armor, on open ground and without cover, took place as the German company was advancing towards Prokhorovka. The battlefield was soon littered with burning T-34s and T-70s. No Tigers were lost and the 181st Regiment was wiped out. Wittmann destroyed eight

A field armored recovery vehicle, based on the Panther hull, towing a PzKpfw V somewhere in the Army Group South sector on the Eastern Front. Twelve *Panzer-Bergegerät* (*Panther I, SdKfz 179*), known as the *Bergepanther*, were built in June 1943 on the MAN production line. Each of the 51st and 52nd Panzer Battalions, operating at Kursk, received four of these vehicles.

Soviet tanks, three anti-tank guns and many other guns on that day (12 July).

In a number of instances, Soviet crews purposely rammed the German tanks. Exploding ammunition could be heard throughout the battlefield. The Soviet 2nd Battalion of the 181st Brigade attacked German tanks positioned on a hill, resulting in many Soviet KV-1s being destroyed by the Tigers. The battalion commander, Captain Skrypin, noted at least three direct hits on a Tiger, but he still did not manage to put it out of action. His tank received two hits, killing the loader and seriously wounding the captain. The driver and radio operator dragged him from his tank, but the gunner remained at his post and continued to fire at the Tiger until he was killed by the following shot. Skrypin took cover in a hole from where he watched his driver return to the burning tank and ram the Tiger. The resultant explosion destroyed both tanks.

The battle lasted until late evening. The Prokhorovka tank battle cost the Germans dozens of tanks, 13 Tigers among them being total losses with another 68 temporarily out of action. Fifteen Tigers were totally destroyed at Kursk. Even so, after nine days of battle, just 43 Panthers were available with most of them in need of repairs.

Assessment

Early reports indicated that, after the failure of the German attack at Prokhorovka, the SS divisions destroyed 70 – 100 abandoned Tigers along with many Panthers. But between 1978 and 1981, after the publication of a number of major works on the German campaigns in Russia, the archives of the Waffen-SS formations that operated on the Eastern Front were declassified.

Careful studies of the daily reports about tank strengths, as well as those of the II SS Panzer Corps, that are preserved on microfilm at the U.S. National Archives in Washington, lead to other conclusions. The Waffen-SS compiled these reports in order to enable corps commanders to estimate the fighting strength of their divisions. The reports, therefore, can be presumed to be fairly accurate. These documents indicate that there were just 15 Tigers in the frontline at the start of the engagement in Prokhorovka and there were no available Panthers in the SS or Army divisions.

The Tiger's performance was known from its previous operations. It is said that on the eve of the battle, Nikita Khrushchyov, then a political commissar, told the Soviet soldiers to memorize the Tiger's disadvantages, "as people once used to memorize the Lord's Prayer." The Tiger might have been few in numbers during the Battle of Kursk, but its crews were able to select targets at will from a long distance, aim, and fire, almost unhampered, at enemy tanks and organized defense positions. The Panther, on the other hand, was still an unknown quantity, even for the Germans. It could face any known Soviet tank, but it was ordered into combat prematurely. The Germans were still encountering problems with its gearbox, steering, suspension, and engine cooling systems. Guderian visited the front between 10 and 15 July and talked to panzer commanders. He was told about the troops' lack of experience and the disadvantages of the new equipment. The too-early engagement of the Panthers at the front brought with it the foreseen results. Guderian later wrote, "they burnt too easily, the fuel and oil systems were insufficiently

One of the initial Tiger models being re-supplied with 8.8cm rounds. Clearly visible are the tank commander's round cupola with observation slits and the "S" mine throwers on the four corners of the hull.

protected, and crews were lost due to lack of training."

That said, the crews were enthusiastic about the new gun as most of the enemy tanks could be successfully engaged from distances between 1,500 and 2,000m. The gun's higher initial velocity gave a straight shot with a small probability of error due to mistakes in the range calculation. Statistics revealed that the destruction of a Panther was equal to about nine T-34s for the Soviets.

Any Panthers recovered after the battle, were sent back to the factory for rebuild. After the teething faults had been ironed out, the Panther proved to be an exceptional war machine, adored by its crews. Later models of the Panther were significantly more reliable than those that fought at Kursk. Without doubt, it was the finest German tank design, with an almost ideal balance between armor, speed, weight, and firepower.

The experience gained at Kursk led the Germans to adopt new tactics. The *"Panzerkeil"* formation did not afford the firepower required to silence deep lines of defense, bristling with Soviet anti-tank guns, so in its place the Germans developed the "Glock" (bell) formation. Panthers led and the lighter PzKpfw IVs followed on both flanks, forming a wide arc, ready to concentrate their fire onto any target. Immediately behind the Panthers were the formation commanders and forward observers for all the support weapons.

The presence of the Tigers in fairly large numbers, as well as the unexpected appearance of the Panthers, revived Soviet thoughts about building new, more powerful heavy tanks. KV production had ended in April 1943. The Soviets started a new program after the Battle of Kursk: that of the heavy "Iosif Stalin" (IS) tank.

The Panthers' and Tigers' superiority over other tank types, even taking their mechanical problems into account, was apparent to both sides during individual engagements. Their low numbers on the battlefield, however, ensured that they were unable to influence the eventual outcome of the German attack against the Kursk salient.

The Reasons the Germans Lost the Battle of Kursk

The battle of Kursk lasted only a few days. It ended in the Germans' defeat – or failure – and essentially "let all hell loose" for them on the Eastern Front, and not only there. There are many reasons behind the German failure. The primary reason was that the German political and military leaders were not in agreement about an attack on the Kursk salient.

General Guderian expressed his strong disapproval of the plan to attack at Kursk.

The Kursk salient was created following the Soviet Army's offensive operations during the winter of 1942-43. The salient had formed in March 1943, when the battles on the Eastern Front ground to a halt. The opposing nations' leaders had different plans for it: Stalin wanted to enlarge it, Hitler to eliminate it. The Soviet dictator, blessed with much more patience than

his German counterpart, waited for the Germans to strike first and then destroy them. And, so it was – his plans were fulfilled.

Many battles are not won by one side but rather lost by the other, as has often been observed. The Germans were defeated at the Battle of Kursk, and in such a manner that it decisively affected future developments. The reasons for the Germans' defeat, therefore, demand analysis.

Paradoxically, it was Hitler's initial successes that lay at the root of the German defeat. The Third Reich's first political and military triumphs were achieved thanks to the Führer's operational intuition: Austria, Czechoslovakia, Poland, Norway and France were all vindications of his personal policies. Germany's military leaders and, indeed, the German people were under the impression that Adolf Hitler never made mistakes. Worse, then, was the fact that Hitler himself also believed in the delusion, which eventually caused him to destroy his achievements and, inevitably, Germany too. Deprived of the right and strength to react, the people and the army stood by impassively as Hitler committed one error after another. The invasion of the Soviet Union was one of his gravest mistakes. Following the initial success and the hardships of two winters in that vast country, it was clear in April 1943 that it would not be easy to win the war. The initial easy advance towards a secure victory had been checked. The *Wehrmacht* lost 1,250,000 men, 5,000 tanks, 9,000 aircraft, and 20,000 guns between

November 1942 and April 1943. At least 100 divisions had been destroyed or were no longer fit for battle. It can be argued that the German leadership had succumbed to an "epidemic of blindness," as no-one saw (or wanted to see) that their future looked bleak.

Another consequence of Hitler's policies, and of the spirit he had instilled in his subordinates, was that his excessive optimism was based on his staff officers' incredibly erroneous assessments of intelligence about the enemy. Hitler's staff had argued that the Soviets had no capacity to launch offensive operations during the winter of 1941 and had proclaimed that the Russians had been taken by surprise at Stalingrad in 1942. Hitler not only took no notice of the actual facts, but he took great care to remove any general who supported a view different from his own. Walther von Brauchitsch, Franz Halder, and Gerd von Rundstedt had all been removed because they had disagreed with him, while Wilhelm von Leeb, Fedor von Bock, and Wilhelm List had been replaced because they had not been able to fulfill his absurd demands.

When such a situation reigns supreme in a military system, the result is failure. The general picture of that terrible war machine of earlier times, the German Army, is vividly described by the British historian Milton Shulman: "Discipline and the chance of a quick promotion made the ones that remained on the German General Staff click their heels whenever the Führer barked. In the meantime, troops at the front were suffering the true agony and hardships from the cold, the fire, and the steel, and all they could do was wonder and obey, because they were too ignorant for anything else." That was the state of the German Army on its way to the Kursk salient.

One of the most fundamental reasons for the German failure was the timing of the battle. Hitler was not particularly enthusiastic about the prospect of an attack in the salient. "The thought of it turns my stomach," he confided to Heinz Guderian. Nevertheless, he considered such a confrontation inevitable. Today it is known that he had been in talks for some time with the Soviets with the aim of achieving a separate peace (just

The grave of Gefreiter Heinz Kuhl who was killed on 21 July 1943. He belonged to Stabskompanie of s.Pz.Abt.503.

The Soviet commander at Kursk, Field Marshal Georgy Zhukov, together with his excellent staff, made all the right decisions, resulting in a resounding victory.

the thought of such a prospect was an anathema to Winston Churchill). The Soviets' final demands were excessive, however, and Hitler, undoubtedly, sought a crushing victory at Kursk to improve his bargaining position.

Hitler's hesitation was shared by some of his most capable generals, including Guderian and Ewald von Kleist. With Erich von Manstein's success in Khar'kov the previous winter in mind, Guderian and von Kleist argued that they had to wait for the Soviets to strike first. They also believed that an Anglo-American operation in continental Europe would be taking place soon enough, and Germany should not become engaged in operations on such a scale, without first determining where the Allies would land. The only logical action on the Eastern Front was to reinforce their lines, gather their reserves and wait for the Soviet attack. Then they could turn the tables with a Khar'kov-style operation. There is little doubt that such a situation would influence the Soviets, and they would prove more reasonable in their

demands for signing a separate peace.

Field Marshals Manstein and Günther von Kluge were the first to show they had "fallen in love" with the idea of the offensive operation. Generals commanding large military formations – army corps, in this case – seem susceptible to becoming intoxicated by the idea of achieving victory against all odds. It was in this way that the outcome of the German attack on the Kursk salient was decided.

A reasonable question would be: was there really some chance of success? It appears that there was one, provided the attack was launched during May 1943, when the ground would be dry after the spring thaw. Today it is known that the Soviets had not yet organized the salient in May, as they were exhausted after the winter operations. In addition, they had sustained tremendous casualties and needed time to replace them. May was the month when the Germans had initially planned to attack, but they later changed their minds and postponed the operation until July, when sufficient numbers of the new Panther, Tiger, and Ferdinand tanks would have arrived on the Eastern Front.

This decision turned out to be fatal for many reasons: a) July was the month during which an Anglo-American landing in Europe appeared most probable, b) the Soviets were given time to prepare and they used it to the full extent, c) a long delay allows more opportunities for the opponent to determine the attacker's intentions (the Soviets knew the exact day, even the exact hour, that the Germans would launch their attack), and d) the Soviets made the most of that time to organize their defense-in-depth concept – with minefields, obstructions, and anti-tank weapons –

Ferdinand tank destroyer at the Battle of Kursk. These armored vehicles did not live up to the German General Staff's expectations. Since they lacked machine guns, the Ferdinands were unable to play a decisive role in close combat and failed to silence Soviet machine guns and infantry defense pockets.

and they continued moving more full-strength divisions into the salient.

The German military leadership disagreed on the use of the new tanks and, as the launch date for the attack was being postponed towards the summer, these disagreements grew louder. Field Marshal von Manstein, who had initially been in favor of the attack, on the condition that it would begin in May, now argued that, "there is absolutely no sense in this operation. The reorganization on the Eastern Front, that has just been completed, will collapse, considering the tank losses to be sustained on it. There is no chance of sending tanks to the Eastern Front and OKH (the German High Command) would have to consider the reinforcement of the Western Front with tanks, so it could face the certain landings in 1944." Manstein proposed, after the May postponement of the operation, an offensive operation through Sevsk or Khar'kov instead of the double attack on the salient.

As for the tanks themselves, on which the Germans had placed so

many hopes, Manstein argued that curing their teething troubles was impossible before the attack. The Ferdinands did not meet expectations, all 90 used in Field Marshal Walther Model's Army were unable to open and clear the way for the infantry. They were also unable to play a decisive role in close combat, as they carried no machine-guns and so could not silence the Soviet machine-guns and infantry defensive positions.

On the Soviet side, the 1943 army was not the one the Germans had faced during the initial phase of the attack on the Soviet Union. The Soviet Army had improved beyond all reckoning when compared to 1942. The large number of American wheeled vehicles (which Stalin saw fit to place as a priority over all other matériel), in conjunction with canned food, had made it extremely mobile. Its leadership, as Liddell Hart once described it, "had been pruned and fertilized," by the previous years' battle experience and its generals and younger leaders had become more tactically proficient.

The Soviet High Command, *Stavka*, had prepared plans for an attack on the Kursk salient, but Stalin was waiting for the Germans to launch their attack first. Contrary to German estimates, the Soviets had retained their reserves almost intact, and would be ready for operations from the beginning of August. The Soviet leadership proved more capable than its opponent in all respects. The *Stavka*, General Staff, and Battle Front Headquarters estimates about the most probable way that the Germans would operate all proved correct. Assessments concerning the approaching enemy operation were unanimous throughout the Soviet hierarchy, something that highlighted the capacities of the Soviet staffs and headquarters at a strategic and tactical level.

Equally successful was the conduct of the battle by Field Marshal Georgy Konstantinovich Zhukov and his staff. In his memoirs, the Soviet Field Marshal denies rumors that Stalin alone took all final decisions of a military and strategic nature. It was Zhukov who directed the battle, although in one instance, *Stavka*, which was always very well informed, ordered him to move to the area of Prokhorovka in order to coordinate the operations on the Voronezh and Steppe Fronts. Field Marshal Zhukov had proven the Soviet Army's ability to conduct strategic defense operations against a well-equipped adversary and its ability to launch a pre-planned strategic offensive operation once the defensive battle had been won.

In contrast, the German high command revealed its weakness yet again. Hitler, like the British General Douglas Haig during World War I, relied on the number of divisions at his disposal. The divisions enumerated in his paper battle plans were, in many cases, of reduced strength, however. The missing troops (those killed or wounded in the fierce battles of the Eastern Front) had been the cream of their fighting manpower. In addition, many of these divisions were merely dots on the map as they had been lost on the Volga, in the Caucasus, and Tunisia. The Germans planned to strike the Soviets at their strongest point, as Bernard Montgomery had done to them at the Battle of El-Alamein. But there was a difference: Montgomery possessed infinitely more means than his opponent. In the case of Kursk, the Germans were inferior to their adversary in all departments.

Another major factor was the inflexibility of the German command structure: everything started and ended with Hitler. There was no unified command during the battle. It is true that attempts were made to appoint a Commander-in-Chief to better direct the battle, but all the proposals were turned down with various excuses, mostly unfounded. All the military leaders were below Hitler in the hierarchy, right down to the last soldier, and could only obey and execute. In the end, Hitler did not hesitate to attribute the failure to the fact that his generals had proven that they had no faith in him and his power of will!

The primary feature of this great battle was that the outcome was not decided by the tactical and strategic capabilities of the respective leaders, but by the mass of matériel (predominantly armor) and the density of the obstructions on the one hand, and to the principle of economy of forces on the other. The Soviets proved they had infinite manpower but, nevertheless, they avoided launching untimely attacks, as they knew that the matériel at the disposal of their armored troops and tank divisions was not infinite. Instead, they waited for their opponent to exhaust himself first and for the Anglo-American landings in Sicily that took place on 10 July 1943.

The Germans sent out their precious panzers to try to break through heavily fortified positions, without sufficiently coordinating their advance with the infantry, the artillery, or the air force. The Germans also underestimated their "racially inferior" opponent. In consequence, many panzer divisions were destroyed for what was in the final analysis an insignificant objective. From the moment the Battle of Kursk was lost, the role of the German panzer forces was restricted to mobile defense and local counterattacks.

If the Germans' objective in the Battle of Kursk is defined as insignificant, what makes this battle one of the most decisive of World War II? In no way can this battle be compared with the really grand drama at the gates of Moscow in 1941. While about 20 panzer divisions were terribly mauled, their Soviet counterparts also paid an enormous price. The Soviet Union, however, was in a position to replace its losses. Guderian had predicted that such a loss would be catastrophic. The overall planning of the operations was erroneous in that the tactical objectives were not well chosen and, in consequence, the Germans lost their chance for a strategic success. While the defeats in the suburbs of Moscow and Stalingrad had seriously wounded the *Wehrmacht*, Germany did not then lose the strategic initiative on the Eastern Front. After Kursk, however, Germany did lose the

Field Marshal Erich von Manstein, in the case of Kursk, was unable to pull off one of his usual "miracles" and reap victory for the Germans.

initiative, and it is this fact that makes Kursk decisive. The German Army began falling back after August 1943, but it continued fighting, although the Germans knew that, in the end, they would lose the war. At the same time, the Soviet Army started its great offensive comeback, driving the Germans from Soviet soil and reaching to the heart of Germany.

Field Marshal Zhukov's words on the final conclusion of the battle are worth noting: "What was the decisive factor for the enemy's defeat close to Kursk? What caused this great attack that had been prepared for so long to fail?" The Soviet Field Marshal does not consider, as decisive factors, the prior knowledge of the enemy's plans, the Soviet superiority in matériel, or Russian efficiency in directing the battle. "More than anything else, once the defensive battle began, the Soviet troops proved superior to those of the enemy, not only in numbers but, especially, in quality."

Rare Photos of Selected Soviet Equipment Used in the Battle of Kursk

The Battle of Kursk was the greatest tank battle in history and practically the last great German attempt to check the Soviet Army's counterattack on the Eastern Front. Tanks on both sides, naturally played a leading role, but artillery – especially Soviet artillery – was also decisive for the conclusion of the confrontation. Here is a selection of Soviet equipment used during the battle.

A Soviet BM-13-16 *Katyusha* multiple rocket launcher mounted on the chassis of an American 5-ton truck manufactured by the Studebaker Company (Studebaker US6). It was able to launch sixteen 132mm Type M-13 rockets with a range of around 8.5km.

The excellent Soviet 120mm PM38 mortar, also used by the German Army in their thousands from captured Soviet stocks. The Germans built an exact copy, the sGrW 42, which entered service at the end of 1942. Total German production of this mortar was around 8,500 tubes between 1942 and 1945. It had a range of approximately 6,000m. The Soviets used the 120mm mortars extensively throughout the Battle of Kursk.

Soviet 7.62mm PM 1910 medium machine-gun on the left with its replacement, the 7.62mm SG 43 Goryunov, on the right. Its wheel-mounted tripod was a lighter version of the Sokolov tripod. The Soviet Army took delivery of the first SG 43s in May 1943.

The Soviet KV-1 Model 1941 heavy tank fitted with a welded turret. It possessed thick armor, a 76.2mm gun and carried a crew of five. More than 5,000 KV tanks of all types were built between 1939 and 1943. These tanks were used during the Battle of Kursk, but the appearance of the German Panthers and Tigers quickly proved that the type had become obsolete. The IS-2 heavy tank was the KV-1's replacement.

A T-34/76 Model 1943, with the new hexagonal turret and additional armor. Most of the T-34s were this variant. The gun was identical to that used on the Model 1941-1942 T-34/76: the 76.2mm F-34L L/42. The Battle of Kursk was the T-34/76s swansong as its deficiencies in the face of the newly introduced German Tigers and Panthers quickly became apparent.

The 57mm anti-tank gun (57mm ZIS-2) Model 1943. It weighed 1,250kg, had an elevation of between -5 to +25 degrees, a maximum range of 8,400m and rate of fire of 15 rounds per minute. It entered service during the summer of 1943. Note the length of the barrel.

The SU-76 76.2mm self-propelled gun was the product of mounting the 76.2mm ZIS-3 gun on the hull of the T-70 light tank. It entered production at the end of 1942. It had a crew of four and weighed 11 tons, but its armor was only 25mm thick. Its open fighting compartment created problems for the crews and was its major disadvantage. In addition, it was under-armored. Although initially designed as a tank destroyer, it was finally used as a self-propelled gun.

A quarter of all heavy machine-guns on the frontline plus over half of those in the rear were assigned for use as anti-aircraft weapons. Shown here is the heavy 12.7mm DShk 1938 machine-gun in its anti-aircraft variation. It had a rate of fire of 600 rounds per minute. It is worth noting that there were also other variants, including a two (twin) or four (quadruple) machine-gun mount.

The typical Soviet sniper rifle, the Mosin Nagant 1891/30. The Soviet Army placed special emphasis on this field and 50,000 such special rifles were built each year between 1942 and 1945 (production began in 1937 and ceased in 1963). It had an effective range of around 800m.

The 122mm M-30 howitzer weighed 3,000kg, was operated by an eight-man crew, possessed a maximum range of 11.82km and had a rate of fire of six rounds per minute.

The Soviet Army paid special attention to anti-aircraft protection for its formations during the Battle of Kursk. Shown here is an 85mm anti-aircraft gun (85mm M39). It weighed 3,000kg, had an elevation between -2 and +82 degrees, with a maximum range of 7,600m and fired a round weighing 9.2kg. It could be also be used in the anti-tank role, in which case it was mounted on the SU-85 tank destroyer.

The 76mm M1942 gun (76mm ZIS-3) weighed 1,200kg, had an elevation between -5 and +37 degrees, possessed a maximum range of 13.29km with a rate of fire of 15 rounds per minute. It entered service in the summer of 1943. This type of gun was produced in greater numbers than any other during World War II.

The T-20 Komsomolets tractor unit. Designed to tow 37mm and 45mm anti-tank guns, mortars, and other loads (up to a maximum weight of 1,500 kg), it was armed with a 7.62mm DT machine-gun on its forward right side. Directly behind the machine gun was the gunner's seat, with the driver's seat to his left. It was able to carry six people, three on each side. It was 3.7m long, 1.84m wide, and 1.5m high, and its maximum speed was 50km/h.

The 45mm anti-tank gun (45mm M-42), Model 1942 was a modification of the 45mm M1937 gun, which was based on Soviet copies of the 37mm (37mm Pak 35/36) German anti-tank guns purchased by the Soviet Union in the 1930s. It weighed 625kg, had an elevation between -8 and +25 degrees, a maximum range of 4,500m with a rate of fire of 15 rounds per minute.

Lesser-known Details

● The panzers had, indeed, fallen into such a sorry state following the defeat at Stalingrad that only a charismatic figure of the caliber of Heinz Guderian could reorganize the panzer forces. At the end of January 1943, the Germans had a mere 495 operational tanks on the entire Eastern Front.

● Notwithstanding his bellicose rhetoric, Hitler had not abandoned hopes of reaching an understanding with Stalin. According to Basil Liddell-Hart, a secret meeting between the Reich's Foreign Minister, Joachim von Ribbentrop, and his Soviet counterpart, Vyacheslav Mikhaylovich Molotov, took place close to the front and behind the German lines in June 1943. They discussed the conditions of a possible ceasefire, but negotiations broke down when the Soviets demanded nothing less than the complete withdrawal of the Wehrmacht to the borders of June 1941.

● The intensity of the battle in the northern sector is revealed by the fact that, on 7 July, the German 9th Army urgently requested a re-supply of 100,000 rounds of tank ammunition since its reserves had declined to dangerously low levels.

● A strange phenomenon known as the "Kursk Magnetic Anomaly" was the only reason Kursk was known to the rest of the world before the great battle. Scientists had observed that compasses "went mad" in the area because there were large magnetite quartzite beds (a mineral) below ground. This phenomenon caused a great deal of trouble for the air forces of both protagonists.

● The Soviet military leadership noticed, during the Battle of Kursk, that some units constantly suffered more casualties than others. When the matter was closely investigated, it was found out that the men of these divisions fought wearing the soft side cap (pilotka) instead of their steel helmet. *Stavka* immediately issued a special urgent order to all Red Army units to wear their helmets in battle.

● The Soviets did not hesitate, in the heat of the battle, to launch a cavalry charge against the German 110th Armored Reconnaissance Battalion on the northern sector. The Germans later admitted that they had never seen a more depressing battlefield sight than that of dismembered men and horses thrashing about.

● One of Guderian's first priorities, when he undertook the reorganization the panzer forces, was to request that assault guns be assigned to the Panzer Troops instead of the Artillery, where they had previously been assigned, in order to unify training and modernization of battle tactics. The OKW staff, however, refused on the grounds that "the assault guns were the only way for an artilleryman to win a Knight's Cross."

● The very first day General Kurt Zeitzler took over his duties as Chief of the Army General Staff in September 1942, the OKW Chief, Field Marshal Wilhelm Keitel, privately advised him, "Never disagree with the Führer. Never remind him that at one time he had thought differently on a subject. Never tell him that the facts had proved that you were right and he was wrong. Never give him reports referring to casualties. We have to avoid aggravating his nerves." Zeitzler laconically replied: "When a leader decides to start a war, he has to have the nerves to endure its consequences."

● On 8 May 1943, Hitler was informed that a corpse named "Major Martin" had been washed up on the coast of Spain. Chained to his wrist was a briefcase with the supposed plans of the Allied landings in the Peloponnese, Greece. The OKW "swallowed the bait" and urgently sent the 1st Panzer Division to southern Greece. The deception had succeeded. The Allies, eventually, landed on Sicily in July, and Guderian was forced to admit that, "The 1st Panzer Division was sorely missed in Russia."

● On 12 April, thousands of Soviet citizens responded to the Communist Party's calls to build a new military airfield close to Kastornoye. The first Soviet fighter landed there on the

Lesser-known Details

morning of 24 May. Exhibiting the same enthusiasm, 25,000 locals worked to complete, in 32 days, a 96km railroad line from Stary Oskol to Oboyan', building 10 bridges and huge embankments in the process.

● The 4th Panzer Army began its attack on the Kursk salient by subjecting the Soviet lines between Gertsovka and Belgorod to a tremendous artillery barrage. It was calculated that the German guns fired more shells in 50 minutes than the entire German artillery had fired during both the Polish and French campaigns!

● A few days before the great attack, the Germans invited a delegation of 12 Turkish officers to view the German army, to impress them. They watched exercises of the 6th and 7th Panzer Divisions, whose men had been ordered to shave and put on their best uniforms. Over lunch following the demonstration, the Turks expressed their admiration for the German weapons, but when asked if their country would abandon neutrality to align itself with Germany, they diplomatically replied that the *Wehrmacht* was powerful enough to beat the Soviets on its own.

● The *Luftwaffe* flew more than 1,500 sorties against railroad installations within the Kursk salient during March and April 1943 and a further 4,300 during May and June.

● On 7 July, the Soviet 3rd Mechanized Corps launched a violent counterattack against the *Leibstandarte* south of Teterevino. They would have, in all probability, caught the division wrong footed, but for the lone Tiger of SS Corporal Franz Staudegger, who managed to destroy over 20 T-34s in two hours!

● The Soviets undertook extensive deception measures (*maskirovka*), one of their beloved tactics, before and during the Battle of Kursk. For example, there were 829 dummy tanks in the Voronezh Front area that had been positioned to give a false impression of the front's order of battle to the German intelligence service.

● All the officers of a 20th Panzer Division company were killed in 60 minutes on 8 July, during the battle for Tyoploye on the front's northern sector.

● The German 102nd Infantry Division passed through the town of Sevsk while on its way to attack positions south of Oryol. Large depots of food were seen, recently captured from the Soviet Army. Canned meat, chocolates, even milk and egg powder, all American. The German soldiers, instinctively, lost faith that they could beat the Soviets when they realized that the oceans were open for the Americans to supply them with all their needs.

● Among the problems that most tormented the German troops in Russia during the summer were the lice and flies. Hitler gave orders to his personal doctor, Dr. Theo Morell, to make a special powder against psoriasis, called "Lauseto," which was produced in great quantities and distributed to the troops, bringing in a great financial reward to its inventor. It was not long, however, before the troops realized that this new product was virtually useless.

● Monday, 5 July 1943 was probably the deadliest day of World War II in the air, with regard to the number of aircraft shot down. The *Luftwaffe* claimed 432 Soviet aircraft destroyed while the Russians claimed a slightly lower figure.

● The der Führer Regiment used six Russian deserters to intercept and translate the signal traffic between the Soviet units. On 8 July, they informed the Germans that great confusion reigned in some enemy units. In consequence, the Germans sent a company that managed to surprise and capture a Soviet colonel along with his entire staff.

● The *Das Führer* Division used six Russian deserters to intercept and translate the signal traffic between the Soviet units. On 8 July, they informed the Germans that great confusion reigned in some enemy units. In consequence, the Germans sent a company that managed to surprise and capture a Soviet colonel along with his entire staff.

The Opposing Commanders

Lieutenant-General Kurt Zeitler

Son of a Protestant pastor, Kurt Zeitler was born on 9 June 1895. He served as a junior officer during World War I and, in 1934, was transferred to the Panzer Troops. In 1938, as a Lieutenant Colonel in the OKW operational planning department, he contributed to the planning of the military operations against Czechoslovakia. The following year he was promoted to Colonel. He took part in the victorious campaigns against Poland and France, during which he showed such broad perception of mechanized column logistics that General Ewald von Kleist requested his assignment to his staff. He cooperated with Kleist until the beginning of 1942, rising in his colleagues' and Hitler's esteem for the way in which he managed to maintain and supply Panzer Group 1, while other similar formations were forced to slow their advance or became immobilized. Following a personal interview, Hitler promoted him to Major General and appointed him Chief-of-Staff to Commander-in-Chief West (Field Marshal Gerd von Rundstedt). He later turned to him, following the triumphant repulse of the Allied landing at Dieppe, to replace General Franz Halder as Chief-of-Staff of the Army General Staff (OKW). It was a dazzling leap upward for Zeitzler, who was late in understanding that Hitler simply wanted to have a "man of action" next to him, rather than a theoretician who would interrupt him with continuous objections. Zeitzler, called "Lightning" by his subordinates because of his exuberent activity, next turned his hand to the Army's problems. The first order he issued to his staff after taking up his duties revealed his forthright characteristic, "I demand that the General Staff officer radiate faith. Faith in the Führer, faith in our victory, faith in our work. He must radiate this faith to his subordinates, to the troops with whom he is in contact, and to the commanders with whom he talks." Zeitzler remained in his post even after the failure of Operation "Zitadelle," notwithstanding that it was his own idea. In July 1944, following the collapse of Army Group Center and the imminent destruction of Army Group North, he had a furious verbal dispute with the Führer. This resulted in his dismissal not only from his post but also from the army. Hitler did not content himself with simple dismissal of the general (whom he replaced with Guderian), but also deprived him of the numerous privileges he had as a general. In addition, he was issued with a special executive order dismissing him from the army with the additional proviso that he was refused the right to wear a uniform

Field Marshal Erich von Manstein

Paul Ludwig Erich von Manstein was born on the 24th November 1887, the tenth child of a Prussian artillery officer, Eduard von Lewinski, whose aristocratic family boasted seven generals during the 20th century. While very young, he was adopted by a childless uncle (also from a military family) and given his surname. He was enrolled into the Plön Cadet Corps (a military academy) at the age of twelve, and soon showed himself to be a first-rate student and a brilliant mind, capable of freely expressing his opinion. He graduated from the War Academy in 1914, and in November of the same year was severely wounded on the Western Front. He was awarded the Iron Cross 1st Class and continued his army career in the interwar Reichswehr and, later, in Hitler's *Wehrmacht*. His reputation was heightened in 1940 when, as the Chief of Staff of Field Marshal Gerd von

The Opposing Commanders

Rundstedt's Army Group A, he inspired the sickle-shaped outflanking maneuver that brought about the collapse of France in six weeks. Later, he distinguished himself on the Eastern Front, both as the commander of the 56th Panzer Corps that occupied the Baltic countries in a lighting advance, and as the commander of the 11th Army when it occupied the Sevastopol' Fortress (a feat of arms for which he was honored by Hitler with a promotion to the rank of Field Marshal, making him the youngest in Germany to hold the baton). He was a respected commander, much loved by his troops, and he preferred to carry out his duties close to the front line. He failed to relieve the 6th Army at Stalingrad, but breathed new life into the *Wehrmacht* with his masterly counterattack at Khar'kov in the spring of 1943. This success, however, was later overshadowed by the defeat at Kursk. Although honored with the Knight's Cross of the Iron Cross with Oak Leaves and Swords, Hitler removed him from active service in March 1944, under the pretence that "...the time of the war of movement is gone forever." After the war, Manstein was indicted and charged with war crimes (the most important of which was the "scorched earth" policy in the Ukraine during the withdrawal to the Dnieper River in the fall of 1943) and

was sentenced to 18 years, later reduced to 12 years, imprisonment. He was released on 6 May 1953, whereupon he became a military adviser to the West German Government. He also used his time to write his memoirs under the title Lost Victories. He died on 12 June 1973.

Field Marshal Walter Model

Walter Model was born in Magdeburg on 24 January 1891. Model, whose father was a music teacher with limited income, enlisted in the Kaiser's Imperial Army in 1909 and became a first lieutenant in 1910. He took part in World War I, winning the Iron Cross 1st Class, but suffering many wounds. After the war, the Treaty of Versailles restricted the Reichswehr to just 100,000 men. Model was selected as one of them, but promotions were slow (by 1934 he had reached the rank of colonel). He was a supporter of the National Socialist Party (Nazi) and was first introduced to Hitler by Dr. Joseph Goebbels himself. Model was promoted to Major General in 1938 and served as Chief of Staff of IV Corps during the Polish Campaign and of the 16th Army during the campaign in France. During the invasion of USSR in June 1941, he commanded the 3rd Panzer Division, showing great personal courage,

amazing energy, and an ability to grasp the tactical situation immediately. In October 1941, he was promoted to general and took command of the 41st Panzer Corps and, three months later, the command of the 9th Army. Hitler's faith in Model's worth was not diminished by the defeat at Kursk in 1943. On the contrary, Hitler continued to depend on him by assigning to him the most dangerous missions. The troops gave him the nickname of "Hitler's Fireman," because he was always called on to extricate the Wehrmacht from tough situations. He was promoted to Field Marshal on 1 March 1944 and continued to show incredible devotion wherever duty called him, being awarded diamonds to add to the Knights' Cross. In 1944, it was Model who restored the *Wehrmacht's* Western Front after the storming advance of the Western Allies across France and Belgium. He subjected the British to a bitter lesson at Arnhem, and was the senior commander of the German armies that launched the failed Ardennes counterattack in December 1944. His "swansong" came at the end of the Battle of the Ruhr on 21 April 1945 when he committed suicide, declaring, "A Field Marshal does not surrender to the enemy."

The Opposing Commanders

Field Marshal Georgy Zhukov

Georgy Konstantinovich Zhukov was born in a village close to Moscow on 2 December 1896, and was apprenticed to his father as a shoemaker when still very young. He was conscripted into the Tsar's Army in 1915 and  was a decorated cavalry sergeant by the time World War I ended. He joined the Red Army in 1918, and became a member of the Communist Party in 1919. During the Civil War, he first commanded a cavalry platoon and then a cavalry regiment. By 1930 he was a cavalry brigade commander and, during the period from 1933 to 1937, he was Assistant Inspector of the Red Army, after successfully establishing a number of training schools and writing military textbooks. He commanded a cavalry division during 1933-37 and a cavalry corps in 1937. He emerged unscathed from Stalin's Great Purge and became Deputy Commander-in-Chief of the Belorussian Special Military District in 1938. In the summer of 1939, Stalin directed him to command the Soviet military forces in Mongolia where he defeated the Japanese at the Battle of Khalkhin Gol. He was appointed Commander-in-

Chief Kiev Special Military District in June 1940 and Chief-of-the-General Staff in January 1941. After quarrelling with Stalin, he was punitively posted to command an army group in Smolensk in September of the same year. Stalin, though, later assigned him to organize the defenses of besieged Leningrad, acknowledging his capabilities. He restored order in Leningrad and was recalled to Moscow in October, where his masterly direction of the great battle to save the capital forced the *Wehrmacht* to fall back for the first time in its history. In the winter of 1942, he was made Commander-in-Chief of the South-Western Front, but was soon relieved of these duties to become a highly-placed *Stavka* special emissary for the whole length of the Eastern Front. Under this authority he took charge of the defense of Stalingrad and won its epic battles (after which he was promoted to Field Marshal) and then of Kursk and coordinated the 1st and 2nd Ukrainian Fronts during the winter operation of 1943-44. He coordinated the 1st and 2nd Belorussian Fronts during the battles for the destruction of Army Group Center during the summer of 1944 and took command of the 1st Belorussian Front from November 1944. It was with the 1st Belorussian Front that he captured Berlin in May

1945. Zhukov was made the supreme Military Commander of the Soviet Occupation Zone in Germany (East Germany) in 1945-46 and he became Chief of the Soviet Army for a few months in 1946. Stalin relieved him, however, and he was sent to command the Odessa and Urals Military Districts (1947-52). In 1953, he was made Deputy Defense Minister and, in 1955, Defense Minister. In 1957 he was elected as a full member of the Communist Party Central Committee, but then in October of that year was expelled from all public positions, after fear of his influence and prestige had led to accusations of "bonapartism." Field Marshal Zhukov, the only soldier of the USSR to have won the Hero of the Soviet Union medal four times, died on 18 June 1974.

Field Marshal Konstantin Rokossovsky

Konstantin Konstantinovich Rokossovsky was the son of a Polish railroad worker and a Russian mother. He was born on 21 December 1896, but was orphaned at the age of 14 and began working in the construction industry. He was conscripted into the Tsarist Army and was a cavalry sergeant by the end of World War I. He volunteered for the Red Army in 1918. At first a

The Opposing Commanders

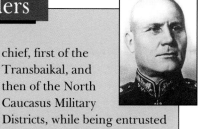

company commander, he became a regimental commander during the Civil War. He enrolled in the Communist Party in 1919 and studied at a number of military schools during the 1920s. In 1929 he took command of a cavalry brigade and the next year was promoted to divisional commander. He was made a corps commander in 1936 but was arrested by the NKVD during Stalin's bloody Great Purge in 1937. He was jailed and tortured for three years to induce him to confess to supposed "crimes against the Soviet state," but was finally released in March 1940 and was restored to the command of a cavalry corps. When the Germans invaded, he was commander of the 9th Mechanized Corps in the Ukraine. In July 1941, *Stavka* put him in command of a large ad hoc formation that was positioned close to Smolensk. During the Battle of Moscow he commanded the 16th Army and, from July to September 1942, the Bryansk Front. His role at the Battle of Stalingrad (he was at that time commanding the Don Front) was decisive, and it was Rokossovsky's troops who eliminated the remnants of Friedrich von Paulus' 6th Army. He was assigned to the Central Front during the Battle of Kursk and took part

in many battles from 1943 to 1945, reaching Berlin as commander of the 2nd Belorussian Front. After the war he was made commander of the Soviet forces in Poland (1945-49), and Minister of Defense and Deputy Prime Minister of Poland. Poland honored him with her field marshal's baton. He was Deputy Minister of Defense of the USSR between 1956 and 1962 and Chief Inspector of the Ministry of Defense from 1962. He died on 3 August 1968.

Field Marshal Ivan Konev

Ivan Stepanovich Konev was born into a peasant family on 28 December 1897. He worked as a lumberjack before becoming an officer in the Tsarist Army during World War I. He joined the Red Army and the Communist Party in 1918, and during the years of the Civil War he served as a political commissar on armored trains (until 1927). He leapt from being a regimental commander to the command of a division in 1932, and completed his studies in the Frunze Military Academy during 1934. From then on, his career was meteoric. Divisional commander in 1934-37, corps commander in 1937-38, commander of the 2nd Red Banner Army in the Far East in 1938-40. He was then posted as

chief, first of the Transbaikal, and then of the North Caucasus Military Districts, while being entrusted by Stalin with the 19th Army during the Battle of Moscow. He commanded the Kalinin Front, the Steppe Front, and the 1st Ukrainian Front, taking part in all the great Red Army battles on the way to Berlin, twice winning the Hero of the Soviet Union medal, as well as the rank of Field Marshal after eliminating the major part of the German forces in the Korsun Pocket at the beginning of 1944. In 1945-46 he was head of the Soviet occupation forces in Austria and Hungary and, in 1946 he took over the coveted post of First Deputy Minister of Defense of the USSR. He then became Inspector-General of the Soviet Army (1950-51), commander of the Carpathian Military District (1951-55), First Deputy Minister of Defense and Commander-in-Chief of the Armed Forces of the Warsaw Treaty Organization (1955-60), and of Soviet forces in the German Democratic Republic (1960-62), at which time he was responsible for constructing the Berlin Wall. After 1962 he was appointed to the post of Inspector-General of the Defense Ministry. He died in 1971.

GERMAN ORDER OF BATTLE

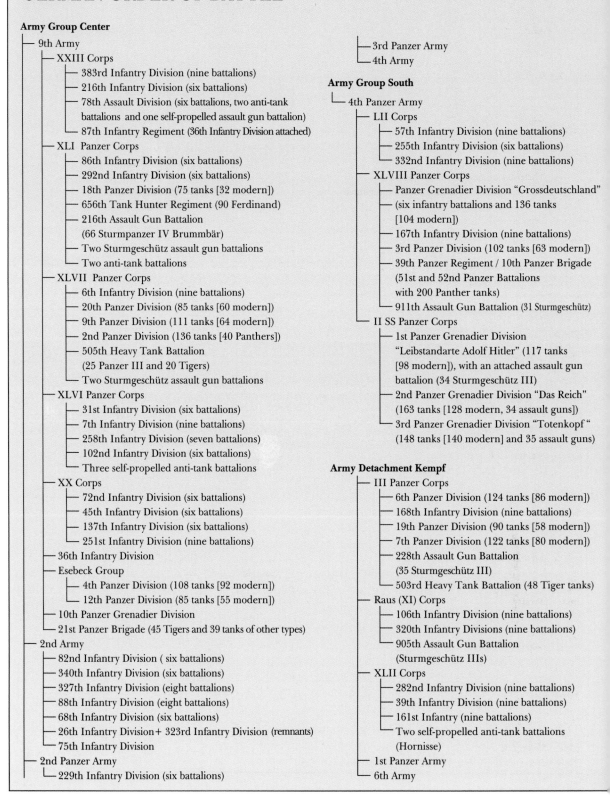

Army Group Center
- 9th Army
  - XXIII Corps
    - 383rd Infantry Division (nine battalions)
    - 216th Infantry Division (six battalions)
    - 78th Assault Division (six battalions, two anti-tank battalions and one self-propelled assault gun battalion)
    - 87th Infantry Regiment (36th Infantry Division attached)
  - XLI Panzer Corps
    - 86th Infantry Division (six battalions)
    - 292nd Infantry Division (six battalions)
    - 18th Panzer Division (75 tanks [32 modern])
    - 656th Tank Hunter Regiment (90 Ferdinand)
    - 216th Assault Gun Battalion (66 Sturmpanzer IV Brummbär)
    - Two Sturmgeschütz assault gun battalions
    - Two anti-tank battalions
  - XLVII Panzer Corps
    - 6th Infantry Division (nine battalions)
    - 20th Panzer Division (85 tanks [60 modern])
    - 9th Panzer Division (111 tanks [64 modern])
    - 2nd Panzer Division (136 tanks [40 Panthers])
    - 505th Heavy Tank Battalion (25 Panzer III and 20 Tigers)
    - Two Sturmgeschütz assault gun battalions
  - XLVI Panzer Corps
    - 31st Infantry Division (six battalions)
    - 7th Infantry Division (nine battalions)
    - 258th Infantry Division (seven battalions)
    - 102nd Infantry Division (six battalions)
    - Three self-propelled anti-tank battalions
  - XX Corps
    - 72nd Infantry Division (six battalions)
    - 45th Infantry Division (six battalions)
    - 137th Infantry Division (six battalions)
    - 251st Infantry Division (nine battalions)
  - 36th Infantry Division
  - Esebeck Group
    - 4th Panzer Division (108 tanks [92 modern])
    - 12th Panzer Division (85 tanks [55 modern])
  - 10th Panzer Grenadier Division
  - 21st Panzer Brigade (45 Tigers and 39 tanks of other types)
- 2nd Army
  - 82nd Infantry Division (six battalions)
  - 340th Infantry Division (six battalions)
  - 327th Infantry Division (eight battalions)
  - 88th Infantry Division (eight battalions)
  - 68th Infantry Division (six battalions)
  - 26th Infantry Division + 323rd Infantry Division (remnants)
  - 75th Infantry Division
- 2nd Panzer Army
  - 229th Infantry Division (six battalions)

- 3rd Panzer Army
- 4th Army

Army Group South
- 4th Panzer Army
  - LII Corps
    - 57th Infantry Division (nine battalions)
    - 255th Infantry Division (six battalions)
    - 332nd Infantry Division (nine battalions)
  - XLVIII Panzer Corps
    - Panzer Grenadier Division "Grossdeutschland" (six infantry battalions and 136 tanks [104 modern])
    - 167th Infantry Division (nine battalions)
    - 3rd Panzer Division (102 tanks [63 modern])
    - 39th Panzer Regiment / 10th Panzer Brigade (51st and 52nd Panzer Battalions with 200 Panther tanks)
    - 911th Assault Gun Battalion (31 Sturmgeschütz)
  - II SS Panzer Corps
    - 1st Panzer Grenadier Division "Leibstandarte Adolf Hitler" (117 tanks [98 modern]), with an attached assault gun battalion (34 Sturmgeschütz III)
    - 2nd Panzer Grenadier Division "Das Reich" (163 tanks [128 modern, 34 assault guns])
    - 3rd Panzer Grenadier Division "Totenkopf " (148 tanks [140 modern] and 35 assault guns)

Army Detachment Kempf
- III Panzer Corps
  - 6th Panzer Division (124 tanks [86 modern])
  - 168th Infantry Division (nine battalions)
  - 19th Panzer Division (90 tanks [58 modern])
  - 7th Panzer Division (122 tanks [80 modern])
  - 228th Assault Gun Battalion (35 Sturmgeschütz III)
  - 503rd Heavy Tank Battalion (48 Tiger tanks)
- Raus (XI) Corps
  - 106th Infantry Division (nine battalions)
  - 320th Infantry Divisions (nine battalions)
  - 905th Assault Gun Battalion (Sturmgeschütz IIIs)
- XLII Corps
  - 282nd Infantry Division (nine battalions)
  - 39th Infantry Division (nine battalions)
  - 161st Infantry (nine battalions)
  - Two self-propelled anti-tank battalions (Hornisse)
- 1st Panzer Army
- 6th Army

SOVIET ORDER OF BATTLE

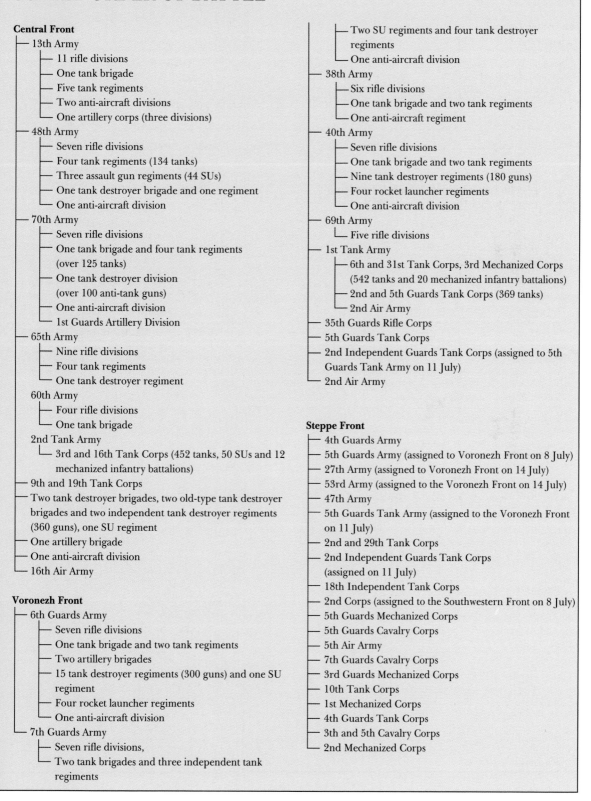

Central Front
- 13th Army
  - 11 rifle divisions
  - One tank brigade
  - Five tank regiments
  - Two anti-aircraft divisions
  - One artillery corps (three divisions)
- 48th Army
  - Seven rifle divisions
  - Four tank regiments (134 tanks)
  - Three assault gun regiments (44 SUs)
  - One tank destroyer brigade and one regiment
  - One anti-aircraft division
- 70th Army
  - Seven rifle divisions
  - One tank brigade and four tank regiments (over 125 tanks)
  - One tank destroyer division (over 100 anti-tank guns)
  - One anti-aircraft division
  - 1st Guards Artillery Division
- 65th Army
  - Nine rifle divisions
  - Four tank regiments
  - One tank destroyer regiment
- 60th Army
  - Four rifle divisions
  - One tank brigade
- 2nd Tank Army
  - 3rd and 16th Tank Corps (452 tanks, 50 SUs and 12 mechanized infantry battalions)
- 9th and 19th Tank Corps
- Two tank destroyer brigades, two old-type tank destroyer brigades and two independent tank destroyer regiments (360 guns), one SU regiment
- One artillery brigade
- One anti-aircraft division
- 16th Air Army

Voronezh Front
- 6th Guards Army
  - Seven rifle divisions
  - One tank brigade and two tank regiments
  - Two artillery brigades
  - 15 tank destroyer regiments (300 guns) and one SU regiment
  - Four rocket launcher regiments
  - One anti-aircraft division
- 7th Guards Army
  - Seven rifle divisions,
  - Two tank brigades and three independent tank regiments

- Two SU regiments and four tank destroyer regiments
  - One anti-aircraft division
- 38th Army
  - Six rifle divisions
  - One tank brigade and two tank regiments
  - One anti-aircraft regiment
- 40th Army
  - Seven rifle divisions
  - One tank brigade and two tank regiments
  - Nine tank destroyer regiments (180 guns)
  - Four rocket launcher regiments
  - One anti-aircraft division
- 69th Army
  - Five rifle divisions
- 1st Tank Army
  - 6th and 31st Tank Corps, 3rd Mechanized Corps (542 tanks and 20 mechanized infantry battalions)
  - 2nd and 5th Guards Tank Corps (369 tanks)
  - 2nd Air Army
- 35th Guards Rifle Corps
- 5th Guards Tank Corps
- 2nd Independent Guards Tank Corps (assigned to 5th Guards Tank Army on 11 July)
- 2nd Air Army

Steppe Front
- 4th Guards Army
- 5th Guards Army (assigned to Voronezh Front on 8 July)
- 27th Army (assigned to Voronezh Front on 14 July)
- 53rd Army (assigned to the Voronezh Front on 14 July)
- 47th Army
- 5th Guards Tank Army (assigned to the Voronezh Front on 11 July)
- 2nd and 29th Tank Corps
- 2nd Independent Guards Tank Corps (assigned on 11 July)
- 18th Independent Tank Corps
- 2nd Corps (assigned to the Southwestern Front on 8 July)
- 5th Guards Mechanized Corps
- 5th Guards Cavalry Corps
- 5th Air Army
- 7th Guards Cavalry Corps
- 3rd Guards Mechanized Corps
- 10th Tank Corps
- 1st Mechanized Corps
- 4th Guards Tank Corps
- 3th and 5th Cavalry Corps
- 2nd Mechanized Corps

Bibliography

Ailsby, Christopher. *SS: Hell on the Eastern Front*. Osceola, WI: MBI Publishing Company, 1998.

Alan Wilson. "*Battle of Kursk, 5th-17th July, 1943 and Kursk – Schwere Panzer Abteilung (Tiger)*", accessed at (http://orbat.com/site/wilson/kursk/ and http://dialspace.dial.pipex.com/town/avenue/vy75/toe.htm.

Armstrong, Richard N. *Red Army Tank Commanders*. Atglen, PA: Schiffer Publishing, 1994.

Basil Henry Liddell-Hart, Sir. *History of the Second World War*. New York: Putnam, 1971.

Basil Henry Liddell-Hart (editor). *The Soviet Army*. London: Weidenfeld & Nicolson, 1956.

Bauer, Eddy. *La Guerre des Blindés: les opérations de la Deuxième guerre mondiale sur les fronts d'Europe et d'Afrique*. Lausanne: Payot, 1947.

Bellis, Malcolm (compiled and published). *German Tanks and Formations 1939-45*. Crewe: M. Bellis, 1988.

Buffetaut, Yves. "La Bataille de Koursk", *Militaria* Magazine, No. 35.

Buffetaut, Yves. "The Panther Ausf. D", *Militaria* Magazine 16, May-June, 1995.

Cartier, Raymond. *La Seconde guerre mondiale*. Paris: Larousse, "Paris-Match," 1965-1966.

Chamberlain, Peter, and Hilary L. Doyle. *Encyclopedia of German Tanks of World War Two*. London: Arms & Armour Press, 1993.

Clark, Alan. *Barbarossa: the Russian-German Conflict 1941-45*. New York: W. Morrow, 1965.

Cornish, Nik. *Images of Kursk*. Staplehurst: Spellmount, 2002.

Cross, Robin. *Citadel: the Battle of Kursk*. New York: Barnes & Noble, 1994.

Donald, David. *Warplanes of the Luftwaffe*. London: Aerospace Publishing, 1994.

Dunn, Walter S. *Hitler's Nemesis: The Red Army 1930-45*. Westport, Conn.: Praeger, 1994.

Dunn, Walter S. *Kursk: Hitler's Gamble – 1943*. Westport, Conn.: Prager, 1997.

Erickson, John. *The Road to Berlin*. New Haven, Conn.: Yale University Press, 1999.

Foss, Christopher. *An Illustrated Guide to World War II Tanks and Fighting Vehicles*. London: Salamander Books, 1981.

Glantz, David M. (Col.) *Soviet Defensive Tactics at Kursk, July 1943*. Fort Leavenworth, Kan.: Combined Studies Institute, U.S. Army Command and General Staff College, 1986.

Glantz, David M. *The Role of Intelligence in Soviet Military Strategy in World War II*.

Novato, CA: Presidio Press, 1990.

Glantz, David M. & Jonathan M. House, *When Titans Clashed*. Lawrence, Kan.: University Press of Kansas, 1995.

Green, William, and Gordon Swanborough. *The Complete Book of Fighters*. London: Salamander Books Ltd, 1994.

Guderian, Heinz. *Panzer Leader*. London: Futura Macdonald & Co, 1982.

Guderian, Heinz. *Anamnisis Enos Stratiotou (Reminiscences of a Soldier)*. Athens: Karavias-Dimitriadis, 1971.

Guderian, Heinz. *Erinnerungen eines Soldaten*. Heidelberg: Vowinckel, 1951.

Guderian, Heinz. *Panzer Leader*. New York: Da Capo Press, 1996.

Healy, Mark. *Kursk 1943: the Tide turns in the East*. London: Osprey Publishing, 1992.

Hooton, Bob. "*Zitadelle – Swansong of the Panzers*," *Armies & Weapons*, 26/27 1976.

Irving, David. *Hitler's War*. New York: Viking Press, 1977.

Jukes, Geoffrey. *Kursk: Clash of Armour*. New York: Ballantine, 1969.

Lehmann, Rudolf. *Die Leibstandarte im Bild*. Osnabrück: Munin-Verlag, 1988.

Mackintosh, Malcolm. *Juggernaut: a History of the Soviet Armed Forces*. New York: Macmillan, 1967.

Macksey, Kenneth. *Guderian: Panzer General*. London: Greenhill Books, 2003.

von Manstein, Erich (Field Marshal), *Lost Victories*. Chicago: H. Regnery Co., 1958.

von Manstein, Erich. *Lost Victories*, Novato, CA: Presidio Press, 1994.

March, Daniel J. and John Heathcott. *The Aerospace Encyclopedia of Air Warfare, Vol. 1, 1911-1945*. London: Aerospace Publishing, 1997.

Milton Shulman, *Defeat in the West*. London: Coronet Books, 1973.

Nipe, George M. *Battle of Kursk: Germany's Lost Victory in World War II?*, accessed at The History Net (http://www.historynet.com/battle-of-kursk-germanys-lost-victory-in-world-war-ii.htm).

Ogorkiewicz, Richard M. *Armour*. New York: Atlantic Books, 1960.

Parada, George. *Achtung Panzer*, (http://www.achtungpanzer.com), accessed in 2003.

Perrett, Bryan and David E. Smith. *The PzKpfw V Panther*. London: Osprey Publishing Ltd, 1991.

Perrett, Bryan and David E. Smith. *The Tiger Tanks*. London: Osprey Publishing Ltd, 1991.

Perrett, Bryan. "Iron Fist." *Classic Armoured Warfare*. London: Cassell, 1999.

Remson, Andrew. *Mine and Countermine Operations in the Battle of Kursk*. Fairfax, VA: Ft. Belvoir Defense Technical Information Center, 2000.

Ripley, Tim. *Steel Storm: Waffen-SS Panzer battles on the Eastern Front, 1939-1945*. Osceola, Wis.: MBI Pub. Co., 2000.

Rokossovsky, Konstantin Konstantinovich. *A Soldier's Duty*. Moscow: Progress Publishers, 1985.

Rothwell, Stephen K. "Bloodbath at Kursk," *Command* Magazine, Issue 36, March 1996.

Scorched Earth. Alexandria, VA.: Time-Life Books, 1991.

Seidl, Hans. *Stalin's Eagles*. Atglen, PA: Schiffer, 2000.

Sharp, Charles C. "Soviet Artillery Divisions in WWII," *Command* Magazine, Issue 34, September 1995.

Shtemenko, Sergey Matveevich. *The Soviet General Staff at War, 1941-1945*. Moscow: Progress Publishers, 1975.

Shukman, Harold. *Stalin's Generals*. New York: Grove Press, 1993.

Simms, Benjamin R. "Analysis of the Battle of Kursk," *Armor* Magazine, March-April 2003.

Spaeter, Helmut. *Panzerkorps Grossdeutschland*. Atglen, PA: Schiffer Books, 1990.

Stein, George H. *The Waffen SS: Hitler's elite Guard at War*. Ithaca, NY: Cornell University Press, 1984.

Sydnor, Charles W. *Soldiers of Destruction: The SS Death's Head Division*. Princeton, N. J.: Princeton University Press, 1990.

Taylor, A. J. P. *The Second World War*. Harmondsworth, Middlesex: Penguin Books, 1976.

Tsouras, Peter G. *The Great Patriotic War – The Soviet Union and Germany 1941-1945*. London: Greenhill Books, 1992.

Weidinger, Otto. *Division Das Reich im Bild*. Osnabrück: Munin-Verlag, 1987.

Werth, Alexander. *Russia at War 1941-1945*. New York: Carroll & Graf, 1986.

Zaloga, Steven J., *The Red Army of the Great Patriotic War 1941-1945*. London: Osprey Publishing Ltd., 1989.

Zaloga, Steven J. Jim Kinnear, Andrey Aksonov, Aleksandr Koshchatsev, *Soviet Tanks in Combat 1941-1945*. Hong Kong: Concord Publications Company, 1997.

Zetterling, Niklas, and Anders Frankson. *Kursk 1943: a Statistical Analysis*. London: Frank Cass, 2002.

Zhukov, Georgy Konstantinovich; Harrison E. Salisbury. *Marshal Zhukov's Greatest Battles*. New York: Cooper Square Press, 2002.

Zhukov, Georgy Konstantinovich, *Marshal of the Soviet Union: Reminiscences and Reflections*. Moscow: Progress Publishers, 1985.